About the Authors

Crystel Lynn Smith

Crystel Lynn Smith, Author, Inspirational Speaker, High-Performance Coach, and Activator was born in a small town in Maryland. At the age of six, her family moved to Middletown, Virginia where she was raised and enjoyed the sense of family and community that her small town offered. Crystel continues to live with her husband, Sean, her children, Brian (Bubby), Stephanie (Luvy), and grandchildren Mason (Mase), Addison (Addy Pie), Ettalynn (Etta Betta) Julius, (Ju Ju Bean) Chloe (Chloe), and Malachi (Mali) in Virginia's beautiful Shenandoah Valley.

Crystel is driven to catapult others to achieve greater than they've ever imagined by uplifting, inspiring, and motivating them, and ultimately activating their dreams!

She has been blessed in her 20-year career with the opportunity to train (lead, motivate, inspire, and propel) over 4,000 people with an extensive track record of success.

While working with hundreds of businesses throughout her career, Crystel became an expert in analyzing business operations, finances, systems, and team (people) challenges and successes. Her expertise, coupled with her ability to inspire, prompted one of the world's largest coaching firms to recruit Crystel as a Business Coach in 2013.

In 2015, Crystel ventured into the world of writing and speaking with her business partner, and friend, Dr. Sherri Yoder, launching her career of passion and the dreams of others to unimaginable heights.

Her reputation for success, leadership, compassion, extensive business knowledge, and strong business and community relationships provided Crystel with the ability to create, and now successfully own and operate, three companies, including Optimum Impact.

Crystel's devotion to revealing and sharing the truth drives her to continue to publish educational and inspirational material as well as travel across the nation, to ignite and fuel the fire that lies within us all!

Sherri Michelle Yoder

Dr. Sherri Yoder, Motivational Speaker, Writer, Learner & Developer, was born and raised in Manassas, Virginia. From an early age, she exhibited a streak of innovation and independence that ultimately led her on a developmental life-course that provided the impetus for her life's work: giving hope and meaning.

Dr. Sherri pursued and completed her doctorate in Clinical Psychology to provide her with the platform to learn about the human experience, and to educate and motivate others to discover and develop paths of accomplishment, enjoyment, and hope in their daily lives.

Dr. Sherri owned and operated a thriving traditional psychotherapy practice, which allowed her the privilege of being invited into the private worlds of hundreds. It was during this time that Dr. Sherri discovered a common thread among all people: the need to connect well and create meaning in every-day life. Her epiphany drove her to dissolve her psychotherapy practice and pursue speaking engagements in the community and in the workplace. Dr. Sherri is passionate about reenergizing the way we view, and protect, our mental, emotional, and relationship health.

Dr. Sherri maintains her Clinical Psychology license in the Commonwealth of Virginia and now brings a strengths-based, positive psychology message to the world. It is her belief that bringing hope and meaning to an individual's daily life will reap the benefits of effective relationships, the bedrock of success.

Dr. Sherri is humbled every morning when she gazes upon a beautiful mountain landscape outside of her home in Strasburg, Virginia. She thrives on building relationships, especially those with her family, friends, and many she has yet to meet! Dr. Sherri is also a recipient of hope. The givers? Her two gorgeous hounds, Leia and Luka!

It's All About Me!

It's All About Me!

Employee confessions!
Everything your employees think, do,
and don't tell you that determines
your success or failure!

Crystel Lynn Smith
and
Dr. Sherri M. Yoder

Crystel Lynn Smith and Dr. Sherri M. Yoder

For information:

Optimum Impact, LLC, 400-B Kendrick Lane, Front Royal, VA 22630

Photography courtesy of Focus on the Valley.

Cover design courtesy of Weathervane Graphics.

Editing courtesy of Kandice L. Thomas.

ISBN-13: 978-1976396342
ISBN-10: 1976396344

First Edition

Dedication & Acknowledgements

We dedicate this book to every person who desires to live a life of passion and purpose: working professionals, business owners, leaders, and those diligently working to create a positive impact in the lives of their families and communities. We intend to inspire you with an understanding of your opportunity to offer your unique gifts to the world through your relationships at work, home, and in the community. And to bolster your appreciation for the inherent value within every person you encounter. We are grateful to the individuals across the nation who boldly shared their experiences for your benefit, and to the many people from whom we have learned who inspired us to humbly be their voices.

-Crystel & Sherri

Table of Contents

Foreword

"The world needs dreamers and the world needs doers. But above all, the world needs dreamers who do." – Sarah Ban Breathnach

Crystel and Sherri are dreamers who do!

Their powerful combination of business acumen and relationship psychology makes them the authority in workplace vitality and the human experience. Crystel and Sherri are pioneers of developing and activating extraordinary lives worldwide!

There has been no comparable message in the thousands of best-selling business and leadership books available today...until now! It's All About Me shrewdly reveals the critical missing elements for today's working world, straight from the mouths of employees across the nation.

You, the reader, will be compelled to reflect and equipped to transform!

Jay Foreman
Best-Selling Author
Second Story Communications

Introduction

In today's workforce environment (a conglomeration of Baby-Boomers, Gen-Xers, and Millennials), leaders and business owners must recognize *and* fulfill the unique needs of every generation, *and* every employee as an individual in their organization if they expect to be successful, or even survive.

The days of hiring based on skillset, dangling the prestigious promotion carrot, and offering traditional healthcare and vacation benefits have long lost their once alluring luster. To attract *and* retain top talent, companies must be aware of employee opinions and be forward-thinking in their efforts to daily optimize their employees.

It's All About Me unveils the powerful impact of employee opinions in today's workforce: the opinions and experience that directly affect your team and company's productivity, profitability, employee retention, and customer loyalty.

Join us to understand how to discover, meet, and develop the needs, strengths, languages, lifestyle, and communication demands of your employees. Empower yourself and your organization with the quintessential insight and tools to create a stand-out, top-performing, sought-after organization in today's increasingly competitive work environment!

Why Me

I am your frontline, your bottom line, your profitability, your productivity, your employee retention, *and* your customer loyalty.

I bet you thought your customers drove those results, didn't you?

I, your employee, am here to tell you that while your focus is on your customers, *I am the one* responsible for driving your four key business outcomes: profitability, productivity, employee retention and customer loyalty.

It truly is all about <u>me</u>. Why?

I am the face of your company.

Your customers look to me for expertise. They count on me to provide an experience that makes them want to return time and again. I can ensure that they continue to come back or *never* come back.

I am the result, good or bad, to all your marketing efforts.

You may generate hundreds or thousands of leads. I am the one who will take those new customers you worked so diligently to get, and I will build relationships, gain their trust, and make them loyal for life, *or* send them to your competitors.

I am the quality of your products and services, great or lack thereof.

Train and engage me, and I will increase the value of your products and services. Expect me to simply "get it," and your value plunges.

I am the service in excellent or poor customer service.

I can engage, "wow" your customers, and set the bar at excellence. If I'm treated poorly, your customers will be as well.

I am the cost of employee turnover and the profitability in employee retention.

Invest in me and I will give you a strong return. Don't invest in me and I will ensure negative equity.

I am efficient or actively wasteful with my time at your company. I want to be efficient and productive.

Give me the proper tools and I will increase efficiency, reduce costs, and increase profitability. Without those tools, I will become frustrated, resentful, and my dissatisfaction will be revealed in the numbers.

I am the voice.

I have access to thousands of your current and potential clients. With a simple click on social media, I can spread the word about how magnificent your company is and grow your business by leaps and bounds. Likewise, I can spread rumors, true or false, about your company that will spread, and burn, like wildfire.

I am dedicated.

I will dedicate thousands of hours to your success every year. I will arrange my family's activities, and even my healthcare, around *your* schedule. Allow me to integrate my life into my work and I will thrive. Tell me to leave my personal life at the door and I will walk out.

I am loyal.

I will commit more than half of my lifetime to your company if I find purpose in my work. Without it, I will become disengaged and merely show up every day, costing you four times that of an engaged employee.

I am innovative.

Give me the freedom to share my thoughts and the ability to implement them, and watch me (and your company) soar. Confine me to your strict policies and procedures and I will wither away in my role, causing you to miss opportunities to become the trend-setter in your industry.

I have unique talents.

Develop them and I will set your company apart from its competitors. Ignore them and I will take my talents *to* them.

I am your employee. And as you can see, it really is all about me!

Teach Me

I, like everyone else I know, want to be successful. I want to do magnificent work. Teach me to do that *for you*!

To be successful every day, I need the knowledge, training, tools, templates, systems, and resources that only your company can provide. In turn, I will give you my talents, skillset, and time. I will add value to your company, your customers, and your bottom line.

Teach me why.

I need to know why my work is important. Otherwise, I will show up every day (or not) merely to collect a paycheck. I will cost you several times my paycheck in absences, time spent searching for a new job, and lack of productivity while I'm there.

Teach me why my work impacts the entire organization. If I don't understand that I am an integral part, I can't, and won't, take my responsibilities seriously. Why would I put forth the effort if it seems to be meaningless work? If I see my work as vital to the success of your company, and ultimately my own, I *will* take ownership and pride in that work. I will meet deadlines and goals with vigor.

Teach me why my work aligns with the vision of your company. Why is it that your company exists? Tell me about your company vision, how you plan to achieve it, and how I will play a vital role. If I don't know what you stand for, how could you expect me to *believe in your organization or my work*? Contrary to what most employers think, purpose and meaning in my work provide more value than my paycheck.

"I used to leave work early almost every day for the last year I worked at my company. I started doing it just to see if anyone would notice. I'm not talking a few minutes early. I mean I'd leave 3 or 4 hours early every day. I was home by lunch time on many days. No one, not one single person noticed. I knew that would be the case. I had only seen my boss twice in the 18 months since he hired me. One day I decided not to go to work at all and, again, no one noticed. I finally called my boss and quit. And I fessed up, explaining that while I like the behind the scenes work, without any communication, my work seemed meaningless. Seriously, what was the point in trying to be productive for 8 hours a day when clearly even the 4 hours a day I put in didn't seem matter? I was shocked! He apologized and said that I was an integral part of their organization, that without my work their system was at risk of being attacked. He said, 'Without you protecting us behind the scenes, I don't think we'll survive long enough to find someone who can protect as well as you do. Or apparently as efficiently as you do!' We both laughed. That was a turning point for both of us. I was given the freedom and flexibility to create my own schedule. I found myself working 8 hours

again on most days, some 12, and some 4. My boss scheduled a regular meeting with me every month. They've really turned into brain-storming sessions. I must make myself go home every day. I want to do more, give more, and protect my company more. I'm so glad I quit that day!"

-Anonymous, VA

Teach me what.

I need to know what is expected of me from *your* company. It is my most basic need. Please be clear and concise. I want to meet your expectations. I want to exceed them. Ask me to explain what *I* think is expected of me, so we can clarify the expectations together. Otherwise, I may interpret them differently and consistently fail.

Teach me how.

This is another fundamental need of mine. I must know how to do my job right. Don't assume that I know how *your* company expects me to get the job done. I must know how I can most effectively and efficiently perform my role. Is there a system that I should follow? If not, create one with me. Set me up for success. Share the tools or templates necessary for me to be productive and accomplished every day.

"I applied for a Customer Service Representative position at the company that I worked for. I was excited! This was a promotion for me. The manager promised me the promotion under one condition: The person who was being transferred, I'll call her Chris, (whose role I was being promoted to), would

train me before she would be allowed to transfer, because he didn't have time. Chris was told that she could transfer to her new office, which was right across the street from her home, as soon as she trained me. She was excited for the transfer because she had two young boys at home and it would give her the ability to go home for lunch and give her about 2 extra hours a day with them without a commute. We were both excited! But what a mess it quickly turned into! She was a _terrible_ trainer. Every time I asked something more than once she screamed at me. She even smacked me in the back of my head in front of customers when I typed something in the wrong field. Chris was frustrated that I wasn't picking up quickly enough, in her mind. It had only been 3 days. I had never done this job before. I had never used this system before. I was still trying to do my job and learn hers. It was so frustrating and embarrassing. On the 3rd day when Chris smacked me in the back of my head in front of customers, I walked out to calm down. She followed me. We got into a heated argument in the parking lot. Yes, there were customers present. I couldn't seem to get through to her and decided to walk in and talk to my boss. He said we needed to figure it out. If we both wanted the jobs, then we both had to figure out how to train me because he was too busy. I decided to take things into my own hands. I asked Chris to stay late and work with me that night. She did. While I didn't know everything, I knew enough to get by. We met with our boss the next day and told him we were ready. She got her transfer and I fumbled for the next month or so. I ultimately taught myself, reading everything I could get my hands on, calling *everyone who I thought may have an answer in the company, learning to read upside-down (while asking clients to sign agreements). I increased deposits by 300% and loans by 700% in just my first year. Then I took what I learned, and my clients, to the competitor. They had a great training process! My entire first two weeks was spent in training. Week one was classroom and week two was hands-on in the office. I was up and running successfully in two weeks! I've since gone on to become a trainer. I'm great at it. I understand how scary it can be. I also know the power in training!"*

-Anonymous, VA

I don't want to say as I've often said, "I was so busy today, but got nothing done." I want to feel accomplished, productive, and proud of my work. I'll need to know how often information changes. I may be the expert in my field, not in industry regulation, compliance, or how they relate to my job. If they change often, I need to know, just as often, to give you the best of me. Teach me how I will receive, where to find, and how to use the updates that are necessary to perform my job effectively, whether they come through email, manual, memos, social media, website, or any other platform.

Let's talk about my results. I need to know how I'm doing. How will *I* measure my results? How will *you* measure my results? If I have and understand those results, I have a sure path to achievement. When you fail to regularly talk with me about my progress, I will flounder and believe you do not care about me. I will eventually leave in search of a company that does.

"I was hired to be a manager. After almost a year of asking repeatedly for, and being promised, management training, I was told that the person who was previously a manager (she had decided she wanted to be a cashier instead over the last year) had changed her mind and wanted to be a manager again. She would be given her role of manager back. However, I would still be responsible for all the daily and nightly managerial paperwork. I explained that paperwork wasn't my strength, that I was a people person. Yes, I could do it, but I thought management was working with people and that's why I applied. During this year I was promised with every passing week that I would be given the promotion, the responsibilities, and authority as a manager. I was excited the first month at my new job. I love to inspire people. I love to serve people. That excitement quickly diminished. Within the first week, two of my employees didn't come to work. I called them both several times. I texted. I waited. I called again. I texted again. I waited some more. I called my manager and he said, 'Give it some time, they're only a couple of hours late,' and asked why I was in such a rush to leave. He said, 'After all, you are getting paid for your time.' Little by little, my devotion was chiseled away. The two employees finally came to work…. the next day. They said they had already talked to my boss and everything was good. I called him to confirm. And confirm he did. I should have quit then. How is it that I could have been promised to have the ability to do

what I do best - lead people - yet the company that offered me that opportunity provided no training, allowed other team members to work when they wanted, and expected me to continue to work while they didn't even have enough respect to call me or answer their phone? It's been almost a year. After watching other employees no call - no show with no accountability, seeing people storm out, screaming obscenities, and quit, only to be called to <u>come back</u> to work, working for minimum wage, I feel unappreciated and taken advantage of. I never received the training they promised. I was never given the opportunity to choose great people to work with. They just didn't care about me... or any of their employees for that matter. So today I cared enough about me. I quit."

-Denise, VA

I must know how I can effectively communicate with my team. In today's workforce of ever-evolving technology and diverse personalities I must find a way to become part of, and communicate effectively with, my diverse team. Effective communication will foster strong relationships for me at work. Poor communication will leave me feeling frustrated, unheard, unappreciated, and unimportant.

Finally, how will I add value to your company with my work? Be specific with me. Saying, "You're a great employee," doesn't cut it. Employee of the month programs "award" me the opportunity to compete with my team for possible mention every 12 months, at best. Sit with me. Lean in. Share with me what talents I specifically bring to your organization. Show me that I am valuable.

Teach me who.

I have a list of people I need to know in your organization. With whom should I partner to ensure my success? To whom should I look for assistance? My role may require different talents and skillsets. If I don't possess them, partner me with someone who does. Trust me. Everyone benefits!

I need to know who my leader or mentor is. If you want me to dedicate my life to your company, you must be dedicated to my personal and professional development. Even professional athletes have coaches. Yes, I am the expert at my craft. Yet, I can be stronger when paired with the right professional partner.

Teach me skillset.

I used to think that I was paid for my time until a great leader said to me: "You are not paid for your time. You are much more valuable to our organization than someone who just clocks in and out. You are paid for your productivity, your talents, and your skills." That, by the way, was a pivotal moment in my career. From that day forward, I shared that story with my team. It's been nine years since I've managed that team, yet they continue to share the power of that story. I may be your hourly employee; however, I want to contribute more than my time. I want to contribute my strengths, talents, and skills.

Teach me the necessary skills for my role. Train me. Partner me with another expert. Mentor me until the skillset becomes my expertise, and I will develop the next expert. We will create an organization of ongoing learning and mastery!

Teach me to access my strengths.

I have unique strengths, although I may not know exactly what they are. I will know when something comes naturally to me. I will shine in some areas and grow dim in others. Sit with me. Ask me what I enjoy about my work. My answers will reveal my natural abilities and you'll discover that I'll invest in developing them because it cannot possibly feel like "work!" There are areas in which I struggle. That doesn't mean I am incompetent. It means that I would be an asset to your company if, rather than focusing on my "areas for improvement," you helped me access and develop my strengths and then cast me in the role that allows me and your organization to shine.

Teach me often.

I despise training to merely gain a credit or check it off the training compliance list. That is a waste of my time, and yours. I need training with a purpose and a plan. Design a plan with me for my continued learning and growth. Then, follow up with me regularly and consistently. If you want me to learn and implement what I've learned, I must be trained and retrained with spaced repetition. Teach me again and again until I've become the master and can teach others.

"Here we go again. Another annual training. Why do I bother going to training? No one ever follows up with me. I always come back to a pile of work. I don't even have time to study, let alone use what I've learned. It's such a waste of time! The company I worked for sent us to a few trainings every year, depending on the 'hot topic' at the office. I usually found the information valuable but challenging to implement. I also found that if I didn't implement what I learned immediately, I didn't retain it. I was tired of wasting my time, and the company's money and time, going to these trainings with no follow up. I thought I would share this with my boss. I asked to meet with him. He was kind enough to schedule a 15-minute meeting with me. I explained that I thought that most of the trainings were valuable and that they would be more valuable and useful if I had a follow-up plan once I returned from training. He responded with, 'Great idea, but I don't have time to do that with you so just get what you can from it and move on.' This training cost the company $600.00 per person. I was one of 11 employees attending. That's $6,600.00 plus the cost of 11 employees out (not producing) for 2 days. You would think that they would want to see a return on their investment and be willing to spend time with us ensuring we, and they, got the most out of it. Not the case. I reached out to the other 10 employees, who were scheduled, to see if they wanted to form a learning team. Seven of them sounded excited about it! I found out that week that the other three were looking for work elsewhere. I thought, 'This is great! My boss will surely be excited that at least eight of his employees were taking ownership of our

learning!' Again, not the case. He said that we needed to be out producing, not relying on each other to learn more. We just needed to get the information and 'do more' with it. Today, three years later, this company no longer has a team of people who want to learn. All 11 have found new working homes. I work for a company now that provides regular training and follow up. I'm learning, growing, and doing! My manager meets with me every week to discuss my progress and to help me continue to learn, implement what I've learned, and grow within the organization. I think I'm going to retire here!"

-Anonymous, WV

Teach me to teach others.

When you teach me, I will be compelled to teach others. Then, I will perfect my skills, access my strengths, impact the lives of my team members, and add value through my contribution to your organization. I will become a trusted advisor to your customers and turn them into raving fans of your company. AND I will have a sense of pride, purpose, meaning, and accomplishment in my work.

"I had never really worked in a sales environment but found myself (after working with them for two years) working for a company that was becoming very sales driven. I really began to worry when I heard that one of my coworkers had been asked to do sales training. I thought, 'I'm never going to be a sales person, no matter how much training they give me. And I hate training. It's so boring!' Boy was I wrong. This trainer

wasn't boring. As a matter-of-fact she didn't even train us. She created a schedule of trainings. On the schedule was every product and service we offered. Beside every product or service was a date and a name. This was OUR schedule. WE were supposed to be the trainers. At first, I thought, 'This girl is lazy. Who does she think she is? She's the one getting paid to train us and we're the ones doing all the work?' The trainer explained that sales were merely meeting customer needs. And that if we knew our products and services we would be able to meet our customer needs easily and thus be great at selling. I had my doubts. But sure enough, she was right! Every week we held sales training. I should mention that she didn't just hand us a schedule and say go for it. She gave us a guideline of questions to answer and then share in the training. The questions made it so easy to learn, teach, and then sell our products and services. They were questions like: How much is the product or service? What are the features? What are the benefits? What scenarios would this product or service benefit the customer? What are some questions you could ask the customer to uncover an opportunity to provide this solution?

We all became the experts and then quickly began to teach others. We were the top sales team of 300 offices that year….and we never felt like we sold a thing. We were just taught to uncover and meet needs. I still work for this company. Any time we hire a new person, the first thing I do is ask them to train me on all the products or services our company offers, with a guided question list, and schedule, of *course. We've become a training ground for all of our local offices and I love it!"*

I am your employee. Teach me and I will thrive.

I will dedicate thousands of hours, possibly years, of my life to you. I *will* play a vital role in achieving your vision. If you don't teach me, I will take my talents, skills, expertise, loyalty, and my return on *your* investment elsewhere. I will take your company insights, customers, and probably even some of your other employees, including their talents and skills, elsewhere. Quite possibly, I'll take them to *your direct competitor*.

Appreciate Me

As a human, I have three basic needs. I need to feel like I belong, that I'm accomplished, and that I'm appreciated. I need these things not just at home with my family, but at work as well. After all, that's where I spend most of my time. Appreciation must be a priority for you because it is for me, and remember...it really is all about me!

Appreciate my presence.

I am a dedicated employee. I come to work so I can make a living. By that, I mean that I really want to live at work! I don't want to just punch a clock, go through the motions, and do it all over again the next day only for a paycheck. I want to thrive. That's why I show up. So, appreciate my presence as an integral part of your team. There are many ways to show your appreciation and I'll talk more about that in a bit. For now, understand that I am here for a meaningful reason, not because I *must* be.

"We BSAs were a loyal and hard-working group. It was nothing for us to work up to 50+ hours a week and only report 40 of them. No complaining, we just did what we had to, to get the job done. There were no rewards for doing that. It's just a trait that all of us shared. Sometimes you had a great boss who appreciated you and sometimes you had a

• • •
21

nightmare for a boss that took every opportunity to belittle you. I still stayed and worked because I had my own work ethic. What broke the camel's back was they were in the process of centralizing the work that was always done by the BSAs. We all could see that by the end of the year, our jobs would be gone. To start that process, they eliminated five of the BSAs and then gave the remainder of us more lenders to support. When a directive was sent out to us, stating that it had been reported by the lenders that they weren't receiving the same level of support across the region from their BSAs (some were more supportive than others), we were told what would be expected of us from then on.

My first instinct was to buckle down and try to do what they were asking. I even went in on my day off and worked to get ahead of the tidal wave that I could see coming. I was stressed to the max and then it occurred to me.... 'Why are you doing this for them? Your job is going away. You'll be 62 in January. Quit!!!' So, I called HR and discussed my options and then gave them a five-day notice that I was retiring. On my last day, our brokerage area called to congratulate me and offer a job with them! I was very flattered and had they come to me before I had made my decision, I would have jumped at the chance, but by this point I just wanted to enjoy being retired."

-Darlene, VA

Appreciate my contributions.

Because you value me, you can appreciate my contributions. You've already discovered that I have much to offer. Now I ask that you don't dismiss my contributions. Instead, appreciate them. Take time to listen to my ideas. Carefully consider them. Then give me meaningful feedback. Whether you take my ideas and run with them isn't the important part. Rather, I ask you to take them, respond to them, and appreciate them. Give me recognition for my contributions to the team, my manager, and our customers. A word of caution though: First, you must find out how I like to be recognized. That's where the "know me" rule comes into play. If you're struggling to know how I like to be recognized, the best thing for you to do is simply ask me. That alone will communicate to me that you appreciate my contributions.

"Management never really listened to most, if not all, of my suggestions or concerns about how to better serve the customers. It seemed to always be only about them and not the customer, in my view. Like they say, 'You don't quit a job, you quit your boss,' seems very applicable in my case."

-Jordon, VA

"I greatly enjoyed the work I was doing at my previous job, but I learned that I desperately wanted to assume the full risk and realize the full reward of my decisions/efforts. The large corporations I worked for weren't going to allow me to do that (as I imagine none would). I started my business in the third year of full-time employment for a defense contractor,

and eventually left to be self-employed two years later. It proved to be a wise decision, and I'm glad I was able to realize the full reward!"

-Marcus, FL

Appreciate me as a person.

I am unique. Yes, I will keep telling you that until you really get it. I have natural abilities and I have natural non-talents. That doesn't mean I'm flawed. It means you've got to figure out what my strengths are and put me in a role where they will be apparent. If you fail to recognize my gifts, you will miss out on "me." You will start to focus on what you deem to be my shortcomings. There's just no appreciation to be found in that type of relationship. Appreciate that I want to offer the world what only I can. Appreciate my need for others to work alongside me who have abilities that don't come naturally to me. Appreciate me as someone who is living life alongside you. Yes, I have a family, friends, responsibilities, and fun outside of work, as do you. Appreciate me in that light and you will appreciate me as a person.

Understand my language of appreciation.

Did you know that we all have diverse ways of feeling a sense of appreciation? I read an insightful book by Dr. Gary Chapman called <u>The Five Love Languages</u>[1]. He talks about how each of us has a basic need for appreciation *and* we have a primary language in which we need that appreciation to be communicated. I encourage you to read it, if you haven't already. I know what you're thinking: *"We're talking about work, not love!"* Well, thankfully, Dr. Chapman teamed up with Dr. Paul White to help us understand how these languages are played out in our workplace relationships[2]. They described the five primary languages of appreciation as Acts of Service, Quality Time, Words of Affirmation, Gifts, and Physical Touch.

Do you know what my language of appreciation is? If not, let's spend some time talking about it.

If it's **Acts of Service**, I experience appreciation when people do things for me. For example, suppose I am your janitor. My job is to empty the trash, dust the desks, vacuum the floors, etc. You, the CEO, because you value me as a person decide to express your appreciation of me by putting your trash where it belongs or cleaning up spills and messes you have made. You know it's my job. You could easily say, "That's what Lacey's here for," and leave trails of debris. Then you wouldn't be communicating appreciation, of course, you would be communicating how little you think of me. Suppose I'm under the gun to get a project completed for you. As my coworker, you could choose to throw me under the proverbial bus when you know there is something I could use your help with to meet my deadline. Or, you could commit an act of service and come to my aid and hence, appreciate me.

What if **Quality Time** is my language? That means I want to spend time with you. I don't want to talk with you only when something is going wrong. I don't want the only time we spend together to be when you are giving me my annual performance review (which in all honesty is likely 6 months overdue). Perhaps it's a conversation in which you and I discuss ideas. Or maybe I want to work with you on a project. Maybe I want to shadow you to learn more about what you do and how you do it. Whatever it may be, it's quality time, not brief nods of acknowledgement as we pass in the elevator or occasional "atta-boys."

If my language of appreciation is **Words of Affirmation**, I need to hear words that affirm and uplift me and my efforts. I've heard my share of the token phrase, "Thanks for everything." You know, the one that the boss tells everyone? Surely you aren't thankful for *everything* I do. Be specific in what you appreciate about me and my efforts. If I close a large deal quickly, tell me, "Wow, Trent, you closed that deal in record time. I'm impressed!" Acknowledge what it is that you appreciate about *me*. I realize being specific takes more effort. You will make the effort if you want me to know that you are sincere. Make it personal. Use my name. Nothing says, "I appreciate you," like knowing my name and taking the time to use it. Feel free to use different means of communication. You can share your appreciation of me in a handwritten note, a face-to-face conversation, praise of me directed to others in my presence, or through an email.

Regardless of your delivery method, make sure it is authentic and specific to me.

Gifts - this one is self-explanatory. If my language of appreciation is **Gifts**, give me something! Since you know me, and know I like turtles, maybe you go out of your way to find a thoughtful turtle gift. Work hard at not giving me something you give to everyone else. Make sure it's something *I* like. I may commute a long way to dedicate myself to you and you might decide to gift me with a gasoline gift card. I might love plaques honoring my accomplishments, so get me a personalized one. You may even decide to gift me with additional paid time off. Whatever the gift, be sure it's a gift you know I want, not one that you would want, and the effect of your appreciation will be long lasting.

Physical touch in the workplace is somewhat taboo and for some good reasons, like sexual harassment. Again, the key here is to make sure that I want and welcome your physical touch. A firm handshake of congratulations might be in order. Perhaps I just lost a relative and you know I'm a "hugger." Ask first, and I'm likely to respond positively. A pat on the shoulder can also go a long way with me. Remember, everyone has their own language. Physical touch isn't for everyone. Always err on the side of caution and ask! I'll be honest with you.

Appreciate me by *using* my personal language of appreciation.

Praise me in my own language. Do it often. Be consistent. I need to be encouraged through appreciation at least once a week. Please don't drop this book now to schedule "appreciation" on your calendar. It is not authentic appreciation, when routinely planned. I ask you to keep an eye out for the things I am doing for which you are grateful. Jot them down if need be. Be certain, however, to communicate them to me. I need you to share your appreciation of me four times as much as you share your criticism of me. Yes, four times. Don't make the dreaded mistake of "sandwiching" your criticism in between pieces of appreciation. I will remember the criticism, not the praise! Your appreciation keeps us focused on my strengths and your success. Appreciating me is a win for you too!

"I had two bosses at my last job. My boss, Herb, made me happy and excited to work! When I went into work, Herb was always ready to work, in a good mood, and super nice. Time always went by fast when I worked with him. He made it a point every day to share every wonderful thing my customers had to say about me like, 'Sammi is so awesome,' and how so many customers said they loved having me as their cashier. I loved working on the days Herb was my boss! My other boss, I'll call her Chris, was a different story. I mentioned to Chris one day what Herb had said about the customers liking me. She said, 'I've never heard that.' Working with Chris was very

uncomfortable. She never had a nice thing to say about anyone."

Appreciate me and I will appreciate you, my team members, and your business! Don't appreciate me, and I will find other ways to feel appreciated, such as helping myself to a pack of copier paper or spending extra time chatting with my friends rather than working. Maybe I'll take my talent to another company who will.

Value Me

Have you ever felt like the "little" guy? You know, the one who seems to have the smallest voice and least impact? Well, sometimes I feel like it's me. It's honestly frustrating, because I have so many great ideas, but I just keep them to myself, because my voice seems to get drowned out by others who have been here longer or have "higher" positions. Let me ask you a question. Has it occurred to you that I, the little guy, just might have valuable input that could benefit you and your organization and you're missing out on it because I'm not on the management team? This isn't a threat. It's an opportunity. When you value me and my contributions, regardless of what position I hold in your company, you will reap an unparalleled level of investment.

"When I first started at my bank, my branch did not have a manager or assistant manager. Frankly, the branch was swimming in the trenches from a lack of leadership. The woman 'in charge' was the supervisor who had been at the bank for over ten years. On day one of being at this branch, she and I did not get along. I am a fast going, hardworking, face-the-problem and fix-it kind of person; where she was a just get-by, only-do-things-to-benefit-herself individual. She would let customers who had large balances do as they please and treat customers with lower balances poorly. She did not support her teller line with decisions and if confrontation arose between me or another teller and a

customer, she would walk into the breakroom. I had my last straw when a customer with a large balance in his account came in and asked for information regarding his transactions. I did not know the customer and asked to see his ID, to which he smirked and responded, 'I don't own an ID, just tell me my information.' I politely explained why I needed the ID and refused to give him information. He yelled for my boss to demand me to give him his transactions. Instead of educating him on the importance of why we get valid ID if we do not know a customer, she snapped at me, loudly yelling, 'This man has millions with us, whatever he says you do!'

I immediately walked away from the teller line and, with so much anger, cried while I called my trainer asking her what I could do. I was amazed at how someone with such a lack of leadership and ignorance could be a supervisor, and had held that position for so long. I remember asking the other employees how she was in the position of a supervisor when she acted the way that she did, and their responses were just, 'What can we do? It's not like if we call HR they will do anything about it. And we can't keep a manager here long enough to care.' After a week, I had had enough.

I began calling HR with every incidence that occurred. I could write a book with the things that she did incorrectly. Of course, she knew the HR people and truly played them well. Once our new manager arrived, he attempted to train her and work with her so that she could be a better supervisor. However, she was adamant on not changing. Why would she? She'd been able to act that way for over ten years. Our manager began contacting HR himself and documenting every incident that occurred. I honestly was at the point of transferring to a different branch or quitting, when finally, after nine long months, she was fired."

-Heather, NC

Value me *and* my coworkers.

Nobody else on the team offers what I do. Likewise, my fellow team members have strengths that I don't naturally possess. Because of that, I ask you to value my team members as well. I experience how you value or devalue me. I watch how you value or devalue my team members. Back-office chatter about one of my team members belittles them...and me. We are a team. We want to experience equity. I *need* equity. When I don't have it, I won't give my all. I'll be less productive, and certainly less motivated. We play a crucial role in the success of your company. Recognize that. I remember working for one manager who seemed to have different rules for different employees. I worked hard because I was in a role that made me thrive. Yet, I continued to observe other employees (who were at my same position and salary level) failing to meet expectations. They were late to work, missed meetings, and failed to deliver on deadlines. Yet, they continued to be a "valuable" part of the team. So, I asked myself: "If I can do *less* with the same outcome from my employer, why in the heck am I working so hard?" You'll lose your best people if they experience inequity. That company lost me. Now it's your opportunity to value us, value me.

"In my 12 years of banking I have worked for a lot of different managers. This one is by far the poorest manager experience that I have ever had. My manager does not back us up, and I honestly don't like even using the term manager when talking about her because she does not depict what a manager should be. For example, when there are customer issues and we are trying to diffuse the situation ourselves, and it is not working, she will not come out of her office to take control of the problem and back us up.

In fact, on many occasions she has picked up her phone and acted like she was talking to someone and when we were done with the customer or task, for which we could have used her assistance, she will just hang the phone up. Another situation that has happened several times is that she would go out for 'officer calls' like every manager is supposed to, but she would never come back and tell us about her experience or who she met, nothing.

These situations made me feel as if she did not value me as an employee/coworker/person. I got the impression from her actions that we were to be left to run the branch while she went and ran errands and drove around town. This manager had absolutely no leadership skills, nor did she know how to do her job or any of the duties in the branch what-so-ever. It makes it very hard to respect someone in her position that would rather sit in her office and look at celebrity news than work with her staff to make the branch grow and bring in new customers. Being in a situation where the person you are to turn to is pretty much worthless, it makes it hard to want to go to work every day and be productive."

-Elisha, VA

Value me by honoring your decision when you selected me.

You hired me, or someone that you trust hired me. If I'm not measuring up, what have you done to honor your selection of me? Will you blame me, or will you commit to making your decision manifest into greatness? What did you see in me when you hired me? Was it my natural ability for clear and concise communication? Was it my skillset or my history of accomplishments? I hope it was a combination of these, because otherwise you hired me to be a warm body, to fill a position that "needed" to be filled. Put me in that role, and I can't possibly thrive or achieve your expectations. I will be just that: a warm body, taking up space, using up your resources, and costing you money. Then you might say to yourself, "Nobody wants to 'work' anymore," or, "I just can't find good help!" You're right. I want to be selected for a role that taps into my natural abilities, so it *doesn't* feel like work. I don't want to have to struggle every day. And you didn't hire me to watch me struggle. That's a headache you don't need. So, value your selections. Value your choice of me by placing me in a role in which my strengths shine. I'll be happy, and you will have confidence in me. You will value me.

"I worked for a company which expected me to do the work of three people. I was also on call 24/7 to ensure their customers had service when needed. I retrieved money for

the company on invoices that needed to be paid and or re-written and submitted. I had employees cuss at me and talk down to me as if I couldn't fulfill the job. This, all being known by the manager and owner of the company. So, it came time for my review, which meant a possible raise. Well how could they not? I had put in a 150%. So, the review is done, and I get a great review! But no raise because I could somehow improve.

I felt so underappreciated, taken advantage of, not worthy, overwhelmed, angry, not valued. I had given them everything I had, even took time away from my family. When it came time to get a little something back, it still wasn't enough. I couldn't believe my manager didn't fight for me, she especially knew all I played a part in. I quit."

-Crystal, VA

Value me by asking for my opinions.

I may not have the length of experience of the "management team." You might see me as an entry-level employee who knows nothing about the industry into which you've brought me. I do, however, have unique thoughts and ideas. Fair warning: they may challenge yours. Value me by taking that risk. Let me share my opinions with you. I need to be heard. I need to contribute. Are there substantial changes coming up? Ask me how it will affect me, my team, and our customers. I have a unique perspective in my role and I'm the only one who can offer it. While you're looking out toward the future, I'm living the present. Value my ability to analyze how changes will affect daily operations. Value me by asking for my opinions about you and about my manager! How long I stay with you, as an employee, and how productive I am while I'm here are a direct result of my relationships with my managers (and ultimately you). Valuing my opinions facilitates the betterment of those relationships...and increases the likelihood that I'll stay, and be more productive, and enhance your bottom line!

"I was at my company for five years, many of which were at times annoying, but mostly okay and tolerable. It was a pleasant enough environment (because of the comradery with coworkers, not management), but nothing to write home about. I resigned because, better offer notwithstanding, if I could list ONE thing, it would be the lack of respect and consideration of my contributions to my company. Sure, I do appreciate the pay which provided a decent living for me and my family, but still it was only a job and not a passion. For example, I thought my view-point was not given serious consideration when discussing a loan scenario, not always, but generally. In meetings, I was often regarded as "invisible", like a plant in the room. I work for their competitor now, who does value my opinion."

-Anonymous, VA

Value me, my coworkers, my opinions, and my ability to do the job you hired me for and I will give you value in return. Undervalue me or see me as just another number in your organization and I will decrease your number of employees by one. Or maybe more.

Include Me

I am on *your* team. If you want me to play a vital role, by utilizing my strengths and talents, I need you to include me.

Include me in our common goal. Include me in your vision.

I need to know my team's common goal and how that helps achieve our company vision. Share the vision with me. Do you know what the vision of your company is? If you don't, how will I know what I am striving for every day of my work-life with you?

Please gather us, your team, and be clear about the vision of *your* company. I'll need to know why you are in business. For a professional football team player, the vision is clear. It is to be the Super Bowl champion. Remember, I'm on *your* team. Give me a vision and I will play a part in achieving it. We will celebrate our win together!

"I'll never forget the day that the President of our company walked into our office and asked us to join him for a few moments. I remember where we were standing, what I was wearing, what the weather was like, and exactly what he said to us. Jim said, as I listened so intently, 'I need your help.' ..... you could almost feel the gasp amongst our team. 'Jim? The President of the large corporation needs my help,' I thought? I listened even more intently. 'We are creating the vision of

our company,' he started. 'And we know that you are the front line of our company. We would like to hear what your thoughts are about our company and what you think describes what our company, your company, stands for and how we can relay that into a company vision that our employees and customers will want to be a part of.' Again, my thoughts were, 'WHAT? They want my opinion? They are including me? The President is including me?' We were an integral part of creating and living the company vision. For five years we lived, shared, represented, and believed in the vision of the company, our company. Sales increased. Employee retention was 100% for all five years at our office. Client retention increased month over month, year over year. We were truly living the dream! Until our company was purchased by another company, a company who did not share our vision, a company who took our authority and required even the most minute decision to be approved by powers that be in other states. We just weren't included. The result.... we **all** quit."

-Anonymous, VA

I am one of several team members. I know that everyone on our team must actively participate and contribute their talents to win. I rely on *you* to rally our team, to provide equity, to give us purpose, direction, motivation, inspiration, and to provide a common goal that unifies us.

When was the last time you shared a common goal that brought us together? Have you given us the ability to access our individual strengths? I've never seen a coach tell a quarterback to just get to the Super Bowl. He would be crazy, right? And probably fired. A strong coach gives the team a common goal. It may be to win a game. Maybe it's to make the first down. These common goals get us one step closer to achieving your vision and feeling a sense of belonging and team unity. The coach, or in my case, *you*, must give us a common goal.

Is our common goal to gain 100 new clients this year? Maybe it is to grow our market share by 10%. Is it to retain 100% of our team? Is it to give 200 hours back to the community through volunteering our time? Whatever you decide, I, and the rest of the team, need to be included and inspired to reach that goal *as a team.*

Include my talents.

Please include my unique talents and the talents of every team member to ensure our success. I have talents and abilities that compliment my fellow team members. Develop them and I will shine. Ignore them and the team will fall short of true success. I will feel as if I've failed the team, and you. I will question my abilities, lose confidence in myself, and probably end up in a discussion with you about my "need for improvement," when the reality is that you may not have noticed my strengths. You may have missed out on my strengths by casting me into the wrong role. The opportunity to win was lost before we even began. My talents were not truly included.

"I was hired in a sales role. I love, love, love sales. Well, it's not actually sales that I love. It's providing solutions that I really love. Sales for this company just gave me the opportunity to provide solutions by 'selling' its products and services. What I didn't know, or should I say what they didn't tell me... There would be a lot, and I mean a lot, of paperwork involved. Remember, I love providing solutions. I never said I loved making copies of papers and filing. I was a top performer, even the top performer world-wide at times. However, with more sales came more paperwork. With more paperwork came more frustration. I asked my boss if we could give some of the paperwork duties to my assistant, who loved paperwork as much as I loved providing solutions. He reminded me, as he often did, that paperwork was part of my job and if I didn't like it, then maybe I wasn't the right person for the job. After five years of being a top performer who was regularly in his boss's office having the 'areas of improvement' discussion...yes, the paperwork problem, I quit. If only they had allowed me to do what I loved and given my assistant the opportunity to do more of what she loved, I may have given them another five, or even 55 years of my life, talents, and production. My assistant was eventually promoted into my role after I left. She was the paperwork lover, remember? She quit after only one year of our boss trying to put her square peg paperwork-loving-self into a sales role."

-Anonymous, VA

Include me in your team.

A team, *our* team, works together to achieve far greater success than each person could achieve on their own. A quarterback would never win a Super Bowl, let alone a single game, with his lone talents. Yet, I often feel as though the weight of an entire goal is on my shoulders. I often feel like you expect me to singlehandedly win the Super Bowl. As a matter of fact, while you incentivize me with an "employee of the month" program, it encourages me to compete *against* my team members and distance myself from them, rather than unite and succeed with my team.

Include me in the vision of your company. Include me in your team. Please be clear with me and other employees about our common goal; our purpose in today's work. If you include, unite, inspire, and encourage us to work together as a team, by incorporating our individual strengths, we will make strides in bringing your vision to life. Exclude me, ask me to compete against my fellow teammates, or demand that I carry the weight, and I will quit your team. Remember, I was looking for a job when I found this one.

Discover Me

There are three things you need to discover about me if you want me to deliver for you all day, every day: 1) My strengths; 2) My personality style in interacting with others; and 3) My language(s) of appreciation. Learn these three things about me and you've made the prerequisite plan for my success as your employee and your success as an organization.

Discover my natural abilities.

By now you've heard me mention the words "strengths," "gifts," "talents," and "abilities" multiple times. In my view, these words are interchangeable. Notice, I did not use the word "skills." That's because talents, or strengths, cannot be taught. They are something that I possess from birth. You can teach me skills all day long. If something doesn't come naturally to me, you will be pouring countless dollars down the drain trying to teach me. I don't want to struggle at work. You don't want to watch me struggle and constantly devise ways to make up for my shortcomings. No, you want to know what my natural gifts are so that you can place me in the role that will ensure my (and your) success.

Suppose you were to answer this question: "What are your strengths?" How would you respond? My guess is you might say something like, "I'm a people-person," or "I'm great at solving problems." Do you really know for sure? What if I were to ask you, "What are my strengths?" Would you describe me in terms of my accomplishments or characteristics? I know. It's a tough question to answer (for now). I'm going to share a tool that will guide you in uncovering my talents (and yours too). It's another book. It's one that I found at a yard sale. Someone clearly had not read it or understood its value. I paid $1.00 for the book and the knowledge I gained is priceless. It's called <u>Now, Discover Your Strengths</u>[3], by Marcus Buckingham and Donald O. Clifton. It changed my philosophy on the meaning of "work." I know it will have the same impact on you. Read it. Reread it. Now, let me tell you how we can put it into action to benefit you and our organization.

Do you want to quickly and accurately discover my strengths? Gallup©[4] has created an assessment called the Clifton StrengthsFinder™[5]. It's a 30-minute, gut-reaction "quiz." It will reveal my top five talents. It will also give us a plan of action to Develop Me. Once you've discovered my talents, you can work with me to develop them and Tailor me to the role that turns my talents into strengths! When you discover my strengths, and give me a role in which those strengths are highlighted, I will be more productive, happier, more loyal, and you will be able to say that you've truly acquired and kept the "talent" you so desperately need to make your organization successful!

"I've been at my current job for five years and enjoy it largely because I have a responsive and respectful supervisor. My longest employment prior to this was not as enjoyable, as the individual who hired me was fired the day before I started, and for two years I was unmoored and totally in charge of my daily tasks, the only psychologist on staff in a very large international school.

I work in an incredibly supportive work environment. My supervisor is familiar with the ins and outs of my job (therapy and assessment and supervision) and she gives me support and guidance as needed, while also letting me go in my own direction. She allows me to carve out tasks that I enjoy to further develop my skills (e.g. She allowed me to take over the assessments at the site and created the Assessment Coordinator position for me, while creating the Group Coordinator for another colleague who has interest and skills in that area). I have flexibility to take time off as needed for self-care and to look after sick kids without being made to feel guilty for taking that time."

-Rachel, FL

Discover my language(s) of appreciation.

I've already talked to you about how every person, including me, has a unique language of appreciation. If you've forgotten, go back and review the "Appreciate Me" chapter before you read on. Most of us have one primary appreciation language. Yet there are those of us who are "bi-lingual," as Dr. Chapman puts it, like myself. Don't worry, this doesn't have to be a guessing game! Dr. Gary Chapman and Dr. Paul White developed the Motivation by Appreciation assessment tool (MBA™)[6], a brief assessment that reveals each person's unique language(s) of appreciation. It is uniquely designed with workplace relationships and communication in mind. This is the best way to find out how I experience appreciation. By the way, you are my leader. I want to know how you prefer to be appreciated as well. Let's take the assessment and find out exactly how to communicate our appreciation for one another in the most effective way.

"I was so tired of getting the standard 'Czar' insurance metal name sticker for the 'Czar of the month' award. Yes, I did great work. I was the ruler of insurance sales. But really? My name on the plaque month over month? I came in early. I worked late. I gave up weekends with my family to exceed client expectations. For what? A name sticker? (17 of them in a row to be exact). All that sticker did was start controversy with my coworkers. There were rumors that I was the 'golden child,' that I must be cheating the system in some way or that I begged people to sign. And it certainly didn't feel like a reward to me. Reward me with something that encourages my coworkers to achieve with me. Or at least reward me with something I enjoy. I'm all about quality time with my family! I asked my manager if I could have a day off since I had exceeded my goal by 36% that month. (It was only the first week of the month.) I explained what my thoughts were about the sticker and shared my idea of time off instead. He

said that I didn't appreciate the prestige of my name on the wall. I agreed. I didn't at all. He apologized. I could tell that he really wanted to give me time with my family. But he didn't. He said that it was company policy to reward people with their names on the wall, not with time off. It took me nine days to find a new job and about four months to transition ALL my clients to my new company, which, by the way, every time I meet my goal, they tell me to take the rest of the day off or even the next day. It's been two years since I've been here and I'm sure I'll be here another 20! They simply get me!"

-Anonymous, OH

Discover my personality style.

No, you don't need me to tell you about my mother or go into intimate details of my formative years. You do, however, need to know my natural tendencies in relating to those around me. In other words, you need to know what makes me tick and how you must relate to me to make our relationship (and my performance) work. There are plenty of personality measures out there that I've seen in the workplace. I've learned that one is particularly effective, yet far too often reserved for those in "leadership" positions. I remember one company I worked for chose to invest in discovery of their employees, but not all of them; only those in management positions. I walked by the conference room where they were busy discovering and making jokes about their personality styles. It seemed like such a fantastic opportunity to bring the team together. Why would they reserve it only for management, I thought? I eventually moved on from that company, but being the learner I am (that's one of my strengths, by the way), I took it upon myself to learn more about what they were up to in that conference room and took what I learned with me.

I discovered the DISC™7 assessment instrument that's primarily used in developing workplace teams. I want to share with you what I learned and why I know you want to provide this learning experience to your team members. According to the DISC™, there are four primary personality styles that directly impact the workplace: Dominance, Influence, Steadiness, and Conscientiousness. I happen to have a primary behavioral style of Dominance. That means that I want results and I deliver quickly. It also means that I can be blunt and come across as insensitive. Why do you need to know that about me? Well, if you want me to do something, get straight to the point. I don't want to talk about your reasoning or learn more about your rationale (unless I ask you). I just want to "do." Your message will be lost to me if you don't communicate with me in the way that accesses how my brain naturally works. In other words, your understanding, and use, of my personality style in our interactions will promote efficiency and productivity. I want that, and I'm certain you do as well.

I also want to know the personality styles of my coworkers, and you! That's going to help me get what I need (to do my own job) effectively. Remember that group of managers in the conference room I was telling you about? They were having so much fun learning about each other. I often heard them lightheartedly saying things to each other like, "You're such a high 'D'!" Man, I wanted in on that fun! This would be a fantastic way to promote team unity, effective collaboration, and comradery. I also happen to know that since I know more about my own personality style, and that not everyone shares my style, I've been able to learn to speak to others in terms of their unique personality style. I've taken the time to pay attention to what they need, and it attracts people to me. The customers happen to notice as well.

"My boss was a High D. Ok, to put it nicely he was a competitive, results driven, get it done now, direct, no non-sense kind of guy. We called him the 'tornado.' He would blow in, give us his demands, and then blow out. My assistant and I were High I's. We are talkers. We love people. There's no such thing as a stranger. So, every day we felt like we just got whipped by this tornado. He didn't seem to care about us at all. He was usually on his cell phone (not making eye contact) as he was giving us our must dos for the day. He never asked how we were doing.

Well, there was one occasion when he asked how my son was. I said, 'Do you mean my daughter?' He mumbled, 'Mmm, hmm,' as he continued to look at his phone. I began to share but was quickly interrupted with, 'I don't need the fluff. Is she ok or not?' I felt like someone punched me in the stomach. For a moment, I had a glimmer of hope and thought that he cared.

My assistant and I, along with two of his other employees have quit. I didn't take the DISC assessment until after I left that organization, and my boss. What an eye opener it has been! Now I know that if someone is direct and to the point I need to be direct and to the point with them. They don't need the fluff. I, on the other hand, like fluffy conversations. Understanding communicating styles has been one of the best things I could have done for my new team!"

-Anonymous, VA

Discover my natural abilities, strengths, language of appreciation, and personality and communication style, and you will discover the unique asset that I am. You will discover that I am not just another employee. I am a person, a person who has immense value to add to your company. When my talents, language, personality and communication style are discovered, you will discover a champion of your business! I will look forward to coming to work every day. I will be more productive, energetic, and motivated. I will share my happiness with you, my coworkers, and your customers. I will be a raving fan and turn your customers into the same!

If you don't take the time to discover all I offer to your company, understand how to show me appreciation, or communicate effectively with me, I will communicate my dissatisfaction, possibly in private, spreading quiet chaos throughout your organization. Chances are that I will eventually share my disdain with you and your company publicly. Remember, I have access to social media and within seconds I can ruin the reputation that you've worked so hard to build.

Develop Me

You've selected me. Now develop me. I want to grow as a person and a professional part of your organization. The more you develop me, the more investment, performance, production, and initiative you will get from me. I can help your company thrive if you help me grow. I can just as effectively make your bottom line shrink if you hire me, train me, then forget about me. Developing me is going to take planning, effort, and purpose. I will match those when you grant me the opportunity.

"I felt valued by my coworkers and the local division. I was appreciated because my work affected how effective the rest of the team was in their jobs. Because I took my responsibilities seriously, the whole team worked together better than they ever had. I took on additional duties because I was not challenged with the status quo and did not have enough duties to do to fill my time, which made everyone else's job easier in the process. I was given freedom to make the job my own and given the tools to do it. Because of my coworkers and the division management, I was torn when I made the choice to move on to a job that challenged me even more and stretched me to develop myself even more."

-Donna, OH

Develop my strengths.

You've helped me discover my unique gifts. Now, let me use them every day. Hold me accountable to utilize them. That means you need to know my strengths as well. Meet with me to discuss how I'm developing them and making them even stronger. After all, I'll be using my strengths for your benefit. Ensure my position is tailored in such a way that it's easy for me to access my strengths and you will be quick to notice them, value me, and express appreciation toward me. Team me up with a coworker who has complementary strengths. Even though sometimes I want so badly to please you, I know that I cannot do it all. I need teammates who can help me achieve my goals. In turn, they need me to achieve theirs. Don't tell me I must do something because it is part of my job if it is abundantly clear that it's a constant struggle for me. Help me develop partnerships with others who will maximize our overall success. Focus on my natural abilities and you will see less error. You will expend far less energy developing my strengths than attempting to teach me one that I do not instinctively possess.

"Can't say I left because of negative circumstances. Well, the president of the company said I'd never make it in sales because I was 'too nice' so I guess that was a thorn in my side for a while and inspired me to start my own business on- the-side. Six months later, the company offered me a big promotion as sales manager for national accounts. Instead of

accepting the promotion, I resigned because my on-the-side business was taking off and I wanted to pursue it full-time. That was in 1995. Three businesses, eight books, and hundreds of clients later, I'm most proud of the fact that I am STILL nice and have not given in to the sales style most companies want where you have to back people into corners until they can't say no. That's just not me."

-Marty, CO

Develop my knowledge.

Give me the keys to your industry by freely sharing information that affects me. Give me educational opportunities that allow me to learn and feel useful. Boost my initiative by providing me with a vested interest in teaching others. Are there new rules and regulations of which I need to be aware? Make time to share their impact on me and the team. Post them on a wall and I'll walk right by without a glance, which might lead me to make a costly mistake for you and the company. I need to know everything that impacts my ability to do my job. And I should have at least a cursory understanding of the knowledge needed by my coworkers to do their jobs. When I ask you a question or look for more information please don't dismiss me. I need that information to do my job the way you expect me to. I'll never be able to thrive or deliver for you without the right knowledge.

Develop my skills.

When you selected me, I had some requisite skills for the job. Training (teaching of skills) is more than just an onboarding process. It is ongoing. What if I told you that I will be successful if you use the following formula: 1% training + 99% reminding = success? Behaviorally, this is a true statement. I've been in far too many jobs in which I have repeatedly failed because of a one-time training approach. I've watched videos and poured over three-ring binders filled with mind-numbing policies and procedures. I've been asked to sign a document stating that I received it and understand it. Well, that must mean that I'll do everything correctly from that point on, right? What happens next? Nothing. I go on to do my job and get an occasional performance review where we talk about areas for improvement. Yet, my skills haven't been developed since I "completed" training. It's not just about repetition, it's about meaningful and applicable repetition. Develop me daily and please don't forget about me. If you do, I'll forget about you too and start looking for a new job like the other 51% of your employees[8].

"Early in my career of banking I had the opportunity to learn and grow with an amazing manager. I had just gotten out of high school and didn't know much about banking, and I could not have asked for a better manager and mentor to help guide me through this journey. My manager wasn't only my manager, we all became a family and since we spent more time here than at home it was a wonderful bond that we made. She always made sure that no one was left behind on

learning policy and procedure, because we couldn't work as a team if we were not all on the same page and have the knowledge that we needed to effectively do our job. One of many things that I will always be thankful for from her is that she pushed us to do the best that we could do. By that I mean that she wouldn't just let us settle for a position, she pushed us to learn everything that was available to us so that we could have every opportunity to grow with our company. As a manager, she took charge and had team building meetings... yes, none of us were excited to get up and be at work at 7 before the drive thru opened or stay late after the drive thru closed at 6 but in the end, it was well worth it and made us a closer, more productive, and on the same page team. We were always made to feel valued and appreciated for our demanding work and this in turn made us work harder toward our goals and have pride in what we had accomplished."

-Elisha, VA

Because you've discovered my uniqueness and necessity to your team's success, it is imperative that you develop me. As you invest in me and watch me grow, I will continue to increase the value of my contributions to you and you will have my sincere gratitude.

Tailor Me

Now that you've uncovered and developed my natural strengths, give me the opportunity to do what I do best every day. I will find purpose and joy in my work. I will be engaged and, therefore, more efficient and productive. I will look forward to coming to work every day. Yes, even Mondays will be exciting for me!

As you can see, uncovering and developing my strengths plays a vital role in my success and yours.

Cast me in the right role and I will flourish. Cast me in the wrong role and I will appear to fail miserably. I say "appear" to fail, because the truth is that I am not a failure. I am talented. I want the opportunity to do excellent work for you.

Tailor my role to my strengths.

One of my coworkers had these five talents: Significance - She needed to feel like she made an impact on the lives of those she served; Futuristic - She had the natural ability to see the big picture that others struggle to see; Strategic - She could formulate a plan like nobody's business; Activator - Once she set her sights on something she had to act immediately; and Command - Wow, did she have command!

When she talked, people listened. They gravitated toward her.

The company she worked for cast her in a sales role where she shined as the number one sales person in their company worldwide. Why? Because she got to do what came naturally to her every day: work with clients to help them fulfill their dreams. However, her manager focused regularly on the fact that her files were not in order. Little by little, with every "need for improvement" meeting, she began to question her ability. Her desire to be at work every day diminished. She lost sight of what a critical role she played as a sales person and focused on making her files as perfect as possible to stay under the radar of scrutiny. The result? She quit. The company lost a great asset. She found a company that valued her strengths and cast her in the role that allowed her, and the company, to shine.

If you are my manager and want me to make your job easy and enjoyable, take the time to uncover my strengths. Sit with me on a regular basis and help me develop them. Then, cast me in the role that allows me to access those talents, and do what I love doing every day.

"I was an assistant to a dean at a community college for a year and a half. During the interview, she asked me what I wanted to learn and grow from being her assistant as well as what I saw for my future. She wrote my responses down and over the course of working with her she sent me to assist various instructors of different programs that had experience

or were doing what I wanted to do. Nonchalantly she would ask me about the conversations that I had had with them and fill in any open-ended questions that I had regarding their field. I didn't realize it until the end, but she was giving me those experiences so that I could see if those fields were right for me and what I wanted to continue to do as a career. I was included on meetings, accreditations, and various program events, respected far beyond a student and employee, and at these occasions given a voice and asked to express my opinion within the conversations.

At the time, I was trying to transfer into UNC Chapel Hill. Being a graduate from there herself, she pushed me, revised my papers and letters that I sent to the school, and included a recommendation letter, that I'm still truly grateful for. She pressed me to go further and to step out of my boundaries to see the bigger picture of what I wanted to accomplish. I still go back and visit her and the instructors of various programs that I had had the opportunity to work for. The dean still goes over those same questions to make sure that I'm still growing and moving forward."

-Heather, NC

Do not promote me to mediocrity.

Casting me in the right role may give me the opportunity for a promotion, but please, do not promote me to mediocrity. Don't dangle the carrots of more money and prestige. Remember, I want to do excellent work. Yes, I want to be rewarded for my efforts. What is most important to me, however, is that I enjoy my work. If I am great in a sales role, don't promote me to a sales manager position merely because of my performance or tenure. I may not have the talents needed to manage people to success. Let's talk about the strengths, not skillset, required for the new role. Remember, you can teach me skillset. You cannot teach me natural talent. Do my strengths align with those required for the role? If they do, I'll be excited for the promotion and I will continue to flourish in your company!

If you promote me based on skillset or tenure, and my strengths do not align with the requirements of the new position, you've just taken me out of my perfect fit. I'll no longer be the expert. I'll no longer exceed your expectations. Instead, you will have promoted me to a seat of, at best, mediocre work wrought with setbacks, frustration, and failure. I can assure you. There are only two possible outcomes. I will quit, or you will fire me.

"I was excited for an opportunity to make more money and get a more prestigious title! My boss said she was moving up in the company and wanted me to fill her shoes. Wow! Me? And fill her shoes, I did. Well, I tried. I'll be honest. I was not good at managing people. It just wasn't, isn't, my strength. I like to be behind the scenes, filing, answering the phones, resolving customer issues, and problem solving. I know those seemed like good skills for a manager. And after all, I had been her assistant for 13 years. I thought it was time I moved up the ladder. Boy, was I wrong. I quickly figured out that my strengths were order-taking and problem-solving, not dealing

with a team of people. I didn't enjoy the weekly calls. I dreaded them. I didn't enjoy talking to people about their 'areas of improvement.' I would make myself sick when I had to let someone go. And often called in sick because I was sick of doing this job. The last day I felt that sick feeling is when my company after 14 and a half years let ME go. They said I just wasn't management material. Duh! I knew that. But that doesn't make me a bad employee. I was a star employee for 13 years. Every one of my reviews was excellent. I was the expert. We had 16 locations. Any time anyone had a question, they came to me and I had the answer. How did I go from being the expert to a terrible employee for the same company? I asked if I could move back to the level of assistant. They explained that the position had obviously been filled and they didn't see a need to add an additional assistant. Blah, blah, blah. It still baffles me to this day. I think I was taken out of my element. I went from being a Rockstar to a floundering fish because it just didn't come naturally to me and admin work did. I didn't really need to work. My husband makes more than enough to support our family. I just continued to work there because I loved it, as an assistant. I'm grateful that they fired me. I've had the opportunity to spend more time with my family, travel, and even volunteer, which I also love. (They just tell me what to do and I do it.) It's just as rewarding as my former job. And they don't even pay me!"

-Anonymous, VA

Tailor my pay to my performance.

Rather than promoting me to mediocrity so I can earn a higher income or have a more prestigious title, place the prestige on my performance. If I do outstanding work, reward me for the same. Give me performance-based pay scales where I can earn more based on my performance. You can create banded pay scales within the same position so that I can grow within the same role. Remember, I am talented, and I *want* to excel. I can become the master of my work. I can perform at my highest level consistently. I will be excited to perform every day.

"I was hired as a part time office assistant, which was all that I desired as a mother of five children. However, soon it was recognized that I was self-directed and had skills beyond what the position required. I was promoted to Office Manager and I agreed to work more hours than intended when I first took the job. I was told that because there was transition at the corporate office with a new HR director, that my pay increase would be retroactive once that person was in place and I would receive prorated holiday and vacation time based on a three-quarter time position. Several weeks later, when that HR director was in place, she did not honor what was promised, did not make the pay retroactive nor give the benefits as promised. Even though I loved my job and coworkers, this always hung over me. I eventually quit."

-June, VA

Recast me.

What if my strengths don't align with my current role? If you continuously talk to me about my weaknesses, think of me as a "problem child," and are consistently creating remediation plans for me, the problem isn't my lack of ability. No, what you've discovered is that I'm in the wrong role and it's time to recast me! Let's talk about it. Don't dismiss me or focus on my "need for improvement." Talk to me. Focus on my strengths. Share the different opportunities within your company in which I may shine. Recast me into one of those roles. You may be thinking, "There's just no role for you here." I challenge you to be creative. If I am talented (and I am), you can use me, and you don't want to lose me. Let's put our heads together to see how we can create the right role just for me. You, the company, and I will all benefit! If recasting or creating a new role is not viable, give me the opportunity to look for a role with another organization. Don't be upset with me if I choose to work for another company, possibly even your competitor. I am only searching for the opportunity to do what I do best every day, to find the right fit in a role that gives me purpose and allows me to add value through my natural talents. Know me as a person and you will want to help me discover my best fit so that I can be a true success. If you have the mindset of "work themselves up or work themselves out," I *will* work myself out at your expense. I will share my dissatisfaction with my friends, my family, and *your* customers.

"I've had some really great 'jobs', some with six-figures ...and I loved many of them. In all my 'employee' situations, I struggled with being a 'team player.' Years of self-examination showed me that while I am excellent in communicating with people and very passionate about my work...I am not, and I never will be, a 'Team Player'; which is often an essential qualification in the traditional work-place. To be clear, in the 20+ years that I've been self-employed, I've found it very rewarding to work <u>with</u> a team of people, but outside the team as a consultant or an advisor.

Everyone is not supposed to be a business owner...and some people are not supposed to be an employee either, but everyone has a passion. Be an employee if you must, but never give up your passion. Follow your passion. Become an expert at your passion...the money will follow."

-Paulette, MD

Tailor my role to my strengths. Tailor my pay to my performance rather than promoting me to mediocrity. Recast me into a better-suited role or allow me to find a new role elsewhere. Those are your best options. I will shine and so will you!

The other options are to allow me to become frustrated or bored with my work, feel resentful for a pay that does not reflect my efforts, and ultimately leave your company, after doing damage during my time of frustration, boredom, or resentment.

Equip Me

This is one of my basic needs. If I don't have the equipment I need to do my job right every day, I will suffer and so will your business.

Too often we hear, "They have everything they need to do their job. They're just lazy," or, "They just don't want to work."

I can assure you that any lack of performance you may see is not a reflection of how much I want to work, or not work. I want to perform. I want, and need, recognition for doing excellent work. To do my job every day, I must have the equipment needed to perform that job.

"I've been given a job to do with no tools and my hands tied behind my back. I've been asked to consider going back to my former job with a promotion. I was told, 'Make the job what you want and the pay you want so you can't say no.' I'm debating that. I do like my current job too. But the fact that the administrator puts road blocks in the way of progress is frustrating."

-Donna, OH

Equip me with the necessary tools.

Give me every tool you and I can think of to make my job easier. I'll be more efficient, productive, and confident in my work. I'm not just referring to tools like hammer and nails or machines in general. Knowledge, for example, is a powerful tool! Up-to-date efficient processing systems, the latest and greatest technology, and even a comfortable climate can be a great tool for my success.

Leave me short of just one tool and you can expect exactly the opposite. I'll be inefficient, less productive, and lack confidence in my ability. Ask me what equipment you can provide to ensure that I can do my job efficiently and effectively every day.   Then, ensure that I have all those tools, all the time.

"We've always been told that the air-conditioning would be fixed when the store was remodeled. It's so hot in here most days, it's hard to think. Our breaks are limited, and we're not allowed to have drinks or fans at the registers. When the contractors finished the remodel after 13 months I was excited to have good working conditions again. I happened to see one of the laborers on their last day on the job and said, 'Thanks for giving us AC again! I'm so excited!' He said, 'Don't get too excited. Corporate said it wasn't in the budget.' I really can't work like this anymore. It's exhausting. I can't even do the job I want to because I'm so sweaty and thirsty. Neither can any of the employees in my department. There

are 26 of us. We're all looking for a new job...with air-conditioning."

-Jane, VA

"Our company had several complaints about our technicians wearing their dirty shoes in their homes. The technicians, myself included, were not comfortable going barefoot in our customer's homes. I recommended that the company purchase shoe covers to give the customers a better experience and the technicians an easy way to exceed our customer expectations. Our management team said they would consider it. That's about as far as it got. We never received shoe covers. Management said it would cost them $36.00 a day and, since they operated 340 days a year, the $12,240.00 investment was too much to justify and their policy was, 'Employees must wipe feet before entering a home.' So, we just needed to do a better job at following policy. I was blown away. After all, this was just another tool that could help me do my job right. And they couldn't justify it? I, we, needed to do a better job at wiping our feet? I knew that day that I would soon be working for another company, one that would provide all the tools I needed. It's been three years, and today I wear shoe covers every day and my customers and some of their _former_ customers love it!"

-Jeremiah, VA

"We have weekly 'how can we do better' calls. Our managers really want to know how they can make the customer experience AND the employee experience better. During one of our weekly meetings, I mentioned that it was very hot, and it would have been nice to have a tarp or tent to work under (we work outside). The next week, we had canopies. I love this company! They are always looking for ways they can do more for us which makes me always do more for them!"

-Brian, VA

Equip me with strength-based partnerships.

If I am great at sales, yet lack filing and organizational skills, give me an assistant that is strong in filing and organizing. Give me the opportunity to seek out co-workers who have strengths that complement mine and allow us to achieve greatness together. Allow me and my counter-strength team members to shine, and we will make you shine.

"I love, love, love how our company encourages us to be who we are rather than putting us in the job description box! Those of us who are the 'creatives,' create, and those of us who are the 'doers,' do; those of us who are 'sellers,' sell. I'll never leave this company!"

-Anonymous, NV

Equip me with on-going training.

Henry Ford said, *"The only thing worse than training your employees and having them leave, is not training them and having them stay"*. Train me. Retrain me. I, we, as humans, learn through spaced repetition. Train and retrain me until I'm the expert and I'll train, retrain, and develop others.

Don't train me and I'll stay, and quietly and slowly wreak havoc in your organization, draining your company profits and morale in the process.

"My current job has elements of a great experience based on the position duties culminating all my previous work experiences into a perfect fit and being personally challenged. I am given freedom to perform my duties without being micromanaged. On the flip side, however, I am given very little guidance or direction when needed. I was shown my desk and told nothing. Had I not prepared for the interview I would not have had any idea where to start. As I like to be self-directed, that has not been a barrier to accomplishing my goals. However, the administrator who has worked in the office for over 30 years and is only working until the perfect time to retire based on benefits, has been a big road block to progress. She does not want change while she coasts into retirement. Much of my job is quality improvement. So, for those responsibilities, I feel my hands are tied as much of the implementation is dependent on her follow through. My challenge is knowing how hard to push or how to go about getting what is needed. Because of being limited in resources and support, it has made a job I love doing, less appealing for the long term."

-Donna, OH

Equip me with technology.

In this day of instant access, our customers, your customers, especially millennials, demand and expect instant results. I must have the capability to meet their expectations. I must have technology that allows me to be as productive and accurate in the shortest amount of time that technology will allow. If older methods, mounds of paperwork, or hours of "downtime" cause me, or your customers, to become frustrated or question my ability, I will question yours. I will find an employer who cares enough about me to give me the technology I need to succeed.

"Our system was so antiquated and slow! Other companies could help their clients in a matter of minutes. I, on the other hand, was tied to the computer for sometimes 90 minutes to handle the same client concern. We lost a lot of clients because of this. I didn't blame them. As a matter of fact, I left that company too, for that exact reason.

I work for a company now (my former company's direct competitor) that understands the importance of technology and efficiency for their employees and clients. WHAT A DIFFERENCE! I feel productive, efficient, and successful every day! And my former company? They've lost several of my coworkers because of their resistance to upgrade their technology.

They always said it wasn't in the budget. I wonder what their employee turnover, dismal employee morale, and snail's-

paced production are costing them. Talk about a budget killer!"

-David, IL

Equip me with authority.

I don't mean to equip me with authority to abuse my power. I refer to the ability to make decisions, based on calculated risk. Give me authority, and I will be the catalyst to your success.

"As a manager, I led a team of 11 employees. I equipped my employees with one powerful tool...authority. I gave every employee 100% authority to make any decision that I, their manager, had the authority to make, given they provided their basis for the decision. I trained them first. Other managers thought I was crazy. They said we would eventually end up 'in trouble,' or getting fired. After all, according to the other managers, I was the manager, the decision maker, the final say, the policy and procedure police, and THE authority. And I had relinquished all my power to the 'lower level' people. I believe there is power in giving away your power! There are no lower level people. There is only us: a small group of people who want to feel accomplished, successful and proud of our work.

It was the best tool with which I could have ever equipped them. We didn't get in 'trouble' or get fired. What DID happen was my team became the expert at resolving issues and ultimately went beyond just problem-solving to developing and implementing proactive approaches to potential challenges. They did not once abuse their authority. They improved customer service. They consistently received raving reviews from customers. They consistently scored 100% on their secret shopper surveys. They exceeded their goals month over month. They came together as a team for the greater good of the company and felt successful, accomplished, and proud!"

-Bruce, VA

Equip me with flexibility.

I do not want to be paid for my time. I want to be paid for my strengths, abilities, skillset, and productivity. You do not want to pay me for my time because, if you do, I will give you that alone. If you pay me for my strengths, abilities, skillset and productivity, I will give you even more. I understand that you have operating hours that require a presence. I need you to understand that I will be more productive, engaged, excited, and loyal to you and your company if you allow me to create my schedule.

Samantha, a local store manager, allowed her team to create their own schedule. She was a true leader and gave them the tools and the training required. The result? The team worked together. They designed their work lives. They could take vacations, arrange family medical appointments, children's activities, and spend personal time building relationships with each other. Samantha's time was freed to excel in her role rather than spending countless hours every week managing the schedule and lives of 11 people. Give me flexibility in my schedule, my practices, and how I accomplish the task at hand, and I will take ownership of my success and yours.

I am your employee. Equip me with everything I need to be successful and fulfilled in my role, and I will equip you for success.

Miss even one tool and I will either stay and do harm, intentionally or unintentionally, to your business or leave for a company who will equip me.

"Both of my experiences come from the same career as a teacher. When I started teaching I was given great freedom to be creative, given the supplies and support needed to do the job. I received positive feedback from parents, volunteers in my room, and a Principal. One volunteer grandmother told me that in her 30 years of volunteering I was the best and most creative teacher she had ever worked with. The Principal would come in my room and sit down. He didn't want to leave. He would tell the children to appreciate me because they may never have another teacher who made learning so exciting and challenging."

But education began to change with No Child Left Behind. Suddenly our freedom to teach was replaced with teaching to the test, testing every 10 days, being held accountable for children who just moved in from a school that was not successful, and we didn't have text books or even basic supplies like paper towels, soap, paper, pencils, etc. Leadership was constantly scrutinizing and criticizing. Test scores reflected everyone's frustration. As a teacher, I felt that they wanted highly qualified, highly educated teachers, but we were being micromanaged, told what to teach, and how to teach to the point of reading from scripts. I quit!"

-Journey, OH

Measure Me

I have a basic need to know how I'm doing. I want to do excellent work, remember? You have provided me with the tools, systems, and knowledge I need to do my job right. You've helped me uncover and develop my strengths. You've cast me in the right role. I am engaged and delivering what I think is outstanding work. I need to be completely sure. And that means that you must measure me and my performance.

Use measurable results.

I need specifics. Whether I am expected to close 10 sales per month, retain 90% of my client base, keep the company restrooms clean to company standards, keep my files up-to-date and in order, offer our customers additional products or services, or maintain OSHA safety standards, I need to have expectations that are measurable. Vague language and expectations like, "Provide great customer service," won't work to improve my performance or even tell me how I'm performing. Remember, our interpretation of great customer service may be different. I will be much more focused and successful with a measurable result such as, "Maintains 95% on all customer surveys." Rather than, "Offers loyalty cards," measure me with specifics such as, "Provide 20 customers a month with a loyalty card." I want to excel and achieve new goals. When you give me specific and measurable expectations, I will achieve them! Leave them open to interpretation and we will both become frustrated. I will share my frustration throughout your organization and with your customers.

Share the tools that you will use to measure my performance.

Could you give me access to a dashboard that tracks my performance? If I am measured with an annual review, give me a copy in advance. Having access to your measurement tools gives me the opportunity to focus on achieving your expectations and feeling successful as often as needed. These tools grant me the opportunity to set a bar of excellence and take ownership of my success. I can make immediate adjustments if I see the specific action needed. If I don't have the opportunity to track my own results, personally meet with me to share the tools you use, and review the results. Then create a system, purchase software, or give me something, so I *can* track my own performance. Trust me, just having the ability to track my own performance will increase my sense of ownership and will ultimately will increase my performance.

Measure me often.

In my experience, it is standard practice for companies to provide annual feedback to their employees, although I have yet to understand why a company would permit me to perform my job every day for 200 or more days before giving me feedback! I need to know how I am doing much more often. Remember, I am on your team. A football coach, for example, never waits until the end of the season to measure the performance of his players. If he did, he would likely be coaching a losing team. I want to be on your winning team! I need your feedback at least monthly and, sometimes, more often. There are times that I will need to be measured weekly. There are times that I am challenged with meeting my expectations and need your feedback and guidance immediately. Yes, I get excited when I accomplish what I've set out to do! And quite honestly, sometimes I'm too embarrassed to ask you for help. The more often we meet, and the more that I see that you want me to be successful, the more likely I am to be open and honest about my needs. Please check in with me on a regular basis to measure my results. It gives me the opportunity to see where and how I can provide even greater value to your company, make immediate changes, celebrate my wins, build trust in you, and feel more accomplished, productive, and successful!

"I worked for a manufacturing company. It was hard work to say the least. But it was rewarding work. Every day I felt accomplished. I worked with a great group of people. Even though I liked what I did, and my coworkers, I had to quit. Every year it was the same thing. Performance review was everyone's least favorite time of the year. We worked hard every day. Yet, the only time our performance was discussed was during our annual review. We used to joke about how we worked 300 plus days a year to hear how we were doing

those 300 days in a five-minute sit down. It finally wasn't a joke after 5 years.

I had processes I knew we could improve. My coworkers and I were always getting better, faster, and stronger. While our performance numbers were above average, our pay was not. We usually received the same annual pay raise that the much slower, low-performing lines received. The final straw was when my review came around again. Yes, I did well. Yes, I got the usual increase. But I wanted to do more. I wanted to share how we did things better and faster on our line. My boss didn't want to hear it. He said that there wasn't a management job open, which is where the process and system ideas come from. I didn't want to be a manager! I just wanted to be the best at my current job. I left the next week, and now work for a company who meets every week with their employees to talk about performance, not just mine but the company's and how I can contribute!"

-Robert, NV

Measure my performance, *not* my lack of ability.

I will be a high performer when I access my strengths daily *and* I am in the right fit. Coaches want every player to be a superstar. They coach each one of them to be the best of the best. Do you want me to be a superstar in your business? Of course, you do. Then I need you to coach me to perform like one. During my performance reviews, focus on what strengths, talents, and skills I have that can make me a superstar in your company. If I need to increase my skillset, or there is an area in which I have the potential to shine, I need you to show me how to get there. Don't tell me, "I need you to get your sales up," or, "You need to provide better customer service." Tell me exactly what my sales need to be and then show me how to achieve those goals like a superstar! If I need to provide great customer service, tell me and show me exactly what that looks like. Is it using the customer's name? Is it answering the phone by a certain ring? Is it getting a 95% on a customer survey? If it's the latter, show me the customer survey.

"My boss used to always tell me that I needed to have a sense of urgency and 'get my sales up.' I hated that conversation. I even asked him how he had been such a successful salesperson. He was such a rock-star sales-person, the company promoted him to Sales Manager. Don't even get me started about that! His response was that he just sold because it was his job. I didn't even know what 'get your sales up' meant. Did he mean more transactions? Did he mean more dollar volume? I asked him those questions too. He said, 'Both.' I finally said, 'I quit.'"

-Joseph, TX

Share your expertise. Guide me in attaining the goals we have set together. Measure me. Give me feedback regularly. Make me *your* superstar!

Reward Me

How should you reward me? I've worked a lot of jobs in which they offered "employee of the month" programs. And I've heard from some of my friends that they are offered a reserved parking spot for the MVP employee of the quarter. What if I ride with someone to work? What if I'm not comfortable with everyone knowing what vehicle I drive? That coveted parking spot is of no value to me. As a matter of fact, that "reward" is something I DO NOT want. What if you have 500 employees? How often will I truly "win" employee of the month? Where is the reward in a name on a plaque every few years or months for work I've done <u>every single day</u> for those months or even years?

Reward me in my language.

I have a specific way that I like to be rewarded. We all do. Have you taken time to read <u>The 5 Languages of Appreciation in the Workplace</u>? If you haven't, get it today and read it. Then, reread it. Then implement it. Make it a way of life in our organization. Remember, first you must discover my language. I may need words of affirmation. Tell me how I'm doing. Tell me what you appreciate about me and my work. My language may be gifts. A gift card to my favorite restaurant may show me that you value me and provide a great reward for my efforts. If my language is quality time, a day off is a great reward. Acts of service may be my language. Organize my files for me. Perform one of my roles for me. Trust me, I will feel rewarded. If physical touch is my language, shaking my hand in congratulations shows that you appreciate and recognize my efforts. You must know my language of appreciation. If you give me a gift card, and my language happens to be quality time, I will resent you for not acknowledging my efforts or even knowing me as a person.

"I was working 60 plus hours a week. I was a salaried employee, so I didn't earn extra pay for my additional hours. I did it because the work needed to be done. I asked my boss if there would be a time where I could earn more time off like vacation or personal days. I just wanted to spend more time with my family. He offered to give me a raise. I literally chuckled out loud. He clearly didn't hear me. I wanted more time with my family, not more money. I asked him again how I could earn more time, not money. I even offered to double my production goals if I could earn time off to spend with my family.

He just didn't get it. I got a congratulatory letter about two weeks later. It was congratulating me on my promotion and raise. When I approached my boss, and said I didn't want more money or prestige, that I wanted more time with my family, he said I was unappreciative of his efforts. I have a lot more time with my family now. I quit and started my own business. And I always ask my employees what makes them happy and makes them feel rewarded for their efforts. Some of them do prefer money, some of them prefer time off. I prefer to give them what's important to them!"

-Kristal, CA

Reward me often.

If you're a parent, think of rewarding your children. You don't wait until the end of the year to celebrate their A honor-roll status, do you? When your child accomplishes something, you recognize it immediately. If you're not a parent, I'm assuming you were once a child. Did your parents wait until you finished elementary school to reward you for your accomplishments over the years? Of course not. I hope not. Remember, I want to do excellent work and I want to be recognized for it. Look, you don't have to give me accolades every day. We, as humans need recognition about every seven days. Once a week, look for, and recognize, the strength, activity, participation, idea, or customer interaction (the gold) I've added to your company every week.

"I have worked for two major companies in my career; the two are a great contrast. The first was a well-known bank on the east coast. They purchased a smaller local bank where I was working as a customer service representative. I was young in my career and looking for a way to transition into a different role that related more to my marketing degree.

The new company, trying to make as many allies as possible, began telling me there would be opportunities for me to get into the different types of jobs outside of a bank branch once the merger was complete. I was so excited! I was fresh out of college and ready to work, excited a bigger company was there to give me a chance at getting out of my home town. But I soon realized it wasn't true. The management team had just said those things to make the initial transition of the merger go smoother. Once the merger was done and the day-to-day activities became routine, it became clear to me that I was a pawn used to encourage those around me to be happy about the merger. The management team never had any intentions of helping me get a different type of job within the new organization. I stayed with the newly merged company for about a year before I'd had enough of feeling used. I was there to meet goals and shuffle clients through. They weren't interested in what else I had to offer.

After I left the bank, I went to a financial firm. The experience has been so different. I've been with the same firm for almost 13 years. Here I am respected, and appreciated. My contributions are noticed. If I have an idea, it is heard and discussed. It may not be implemented and I'm okay with that, because I know it was considered. What makes this management team better than the bank is free; any management team can do these things.

I'm doing a good job, because I'm told frequently. I'm thanked when I spend a long time on a project or when I have to stay late. I get a cupcake just because it is Wednesday, and my boss can tell I've had a frustrating morning. My bosses care about me as a person as well as an employee, which makes me a better employee. I am respected, *promoted, encouraged, and thanked. I am grateful for such a great group of people to work with and have no intentions of ever leaving."*

-Jennifer, TN

Reward us.

The "Employee of the Month" program is possibly the largest demotivator I've seen. Rather than partnering with my team, each of us accessing our strengths, coming together for a common goal, we individually climb over one another, trying to outshine the next. Sometimes we will throw each other under the bus to show that we are the "worthy" ones. This promotes division, not team cooperation. Give us a common goal, a part in achieving your company vision. Unite us. Allow us to access our strengths and come together for a greater good. Then, reward us for our accomplishments as a team. If you are a sports fan, you see this at every game. The quarterback doesn't win the game. The lineman doesn't win the game. The team wins the game, the Super Bowl, or the world championship.

"The owners of our company gave us a challenge to find a way to save them $10,000.00 a month. Our reward was a trip to Vegas for the entire team and our spouses. We found $22,000.00 a month in expenses that we could easily eliminate. Vegas was great! Teamwork really is dream work!"

-Daniel, VA

Reward me as you say you will.

Don't give me empty promises. If you promise a raise after 90 days, give it to me. If you promise me a bonus for certain expectations and I meet them, give it to me. If you tell me I can make my own schedule, allow me to. If you say that I can go as far as I'd like in your company, create a plan for me to go, and then let me. If you make promises only to break them, I will find a way to reward myself. I can assure you that it will be much costlier than simply fulfilling your promises.

"I worked for a medical office. They hired me to do bookkeeping and payroll. This office had a lot of turnover, which I didn't know when I started. It became clear, very quickly, when three employees quit in my first month, a total of 10 in my first year. My bookkeeping and payroll job quickly began to grow to more of an office manager role. I was scheduling patients, invoicing and billing, and answering phones. The list continued to grow as our employee base continued to shrink. We live in a small town, so the word was out that we were not a good practice to work for. Thus, it was hard to replace people when we just didn't have any applications. I wasn't a fan of my boss. He was a yeller and a screamer. But, hey, so was my father, and he didn't pay me to listen to it. So, I continued to work but not without asking for resolution. I practically begged to hire someone to schedule, to answer the phones, someone to invoice and bill…. just someone. The owner said he liked me doing everything because I was so good at it and offered to give me a 4% increase in pay to accommodate me for the extra work. It

wasn't much, especially since I had taken on the role of four employees who hadn't been replaced. I agreed to continue handling everything for another 6 months and he agreed that he would work on finding help. What really happened? He never gave me a raise. He never hired anyone else to help. I asked repeatedly for both over the next year. Finally, I decided to take matters in my own hands. I gave myself a 40% raise, for the next three years. After all, I did do the work of five people, and he did promise me a raise. He eventually found out when the competitor came to town and things got tight. He asked to look at the books. I knew I could be arrested. I didn't care at that moment. I was ready to confront him after all these years. He fired me but chose not to press charges because he didn't want even more negativity surrounding his business. I ultimately went to work for his competitor. I get to do what I love every day, bookkeeping. I asked that they outsource payroll as a level of protection and checks and balances for their company. They reward me every year with a bonus if all the financials are up to date, accurate, and submitted to the CPA on time. You can bet they are!"

-Mary Anne, SC

"During my interview, I asked my boss if I could transfer to a different office if a position opened up. I explained that there was an office within walking distance from my home. I lived at home with my parents who both needed my care, and being closer to home would give me a few more precious *hours with them every day. He said, 'Of course, I don't see why not.' That was a lie. Two years later, a position opened at the office I had longed to work at. My parents' conditions had worsened by this time, so I was super excited to have more time with them. I had to get my current bosses approval to apply for the transfer. I got a letter saying that my application for transfer had been denied. I was furious. He didn't even have the decency to tell me in person. His office was only about 15 feet from mine and I saw him every day. He tried to tell me it was because I was too good at my job and he couldn't afford to lose me. Well, because of his broken promise, he did lose me. I quit that day. I went to a competitor who was within walking distance of my home. I'm still there 10 years later and they've always delivered what they've promised."*

-Ashley, VA

"As an outside salesman, I got tired of being lied to and having compensation 'adjusted' because I exceeded their goals. Plus, some of their 'business practices' were less than stellar. That was 18 years ago, and I'm now happily self-employed."

-Mike, MI

Reward me in my language. Reward me often, as you say you will, and reward us as a team. YOU will reap the ultimate reward of success!

Lead Me

You've heard leadership referred to as driving the bus, herding cats, or managing. The list goes on. If I were to define leadership, it would look like none of these. I'm telling you from my (your employee's) perspective, leadership is not driving, herding, or managing. I believe Kathy Hensley[9] said it best when she said, *"Leadership is being bold enough to have vision and humble enough to recognize achieving it will take the efforts of many people. People are most fulfilled when they share their gifts and talents, rather than just work. Leaders create a culture, serve the greater good, and let others soar."*

Lead me with motivation.

First, you must learn what motivates me. I may be motivated by money. However, I may be motivated by more time with my family, recognition, prizes, promotion, ownership, or purpose. Ask me. Know me, and then motivate me.

"My greatest work experience is when I officially entered the working world and got a 'real job.' I was 19 and about to be a new mom. I was a young adult with no college education. The bank I began working for opened a new branch, and I met Crystel Smith, not knowing she would be the woman who made me who I am today. Her positive attitude, work ethic,

and caring personality made what most would call a job, a second home. As a manager, Crystel taught, guided, trusted, and created a branch of hard-working young people who easily respected and trusted her in return. She gave me the confidence that I have today to believe that I can, and will, achieve whatever goal I set. She was very supportive as a manager, but even more supportive as a friend, and is to this day. The greatness of this experience is that I went to work each day, performed to my best ability, and never thought about calling in sick, or wanting to leave early because I loved my job, my co-workers, and mostly the management. Providing a positive environment with great motivation and praise has always been my expectation when working. I am now 30, have had quite a few jobs, and can finally say I found that excellence in the workplace again. Clearly they are few and far between."

-Stephanie, WV

Lead me with inspiration.

I want to wake up every day inspired to come to work. I may be inspired differently than you are. I may need daily inspiration. Positive videos, big picture discussions, knowing the benefits of my work – these are all things that may inspire me. You'll need to get to know me, really know me, to know what inspires me. Understand this and I will soar. I will come to work with excitement and inspire others!

"Our manager starts every day with a success huddle. Everyone has an opportunity to share their successes from *the previous day. It doesn't even have to be work related. Yesterday I shared that my son made the honor roll. We share daily so we know each other's lives well. My coworkers knew how challenging a few subjects had been for him and how hard he had worked to achieve his honor-roll certificate. Focusing on our successes every morning is a great start to every day, motivate us, and bring us closer as people. We're not just employees and coworkers. We're family and we look for opportunities to inspire each other to be successful at work and in our personal lives."*

-Trent, FL

Lead me by searching for the gold.

Think on this. Those who are successful at finding gold, look for the gold. Sure, they expect that they will have to sift through some dirt. However, they don't look for dirt, and they certainly aren't surprised when they find dirt. They look for the *gold* and, ultimately, they find it! I bring talents to your team. Look for the gold in me, and I will bring the value of my gold to *your* team.

"I was selected to open a new office for our organization. I was new at managing people. I had worked for great managers and not-so-great managers. I wanted to be one of the greats. I knew that finding the right people would be key to my and their success. I only had one request as a new manager with a new office: I needed to personally select my team. My manager was one of the greats. 'Of course,' she responded. During my initial round of interviews, I received a

phone call from another manager in our organization. One of her employees had applied to work at my office. She immediately began to tell me all about this employee. 'Crystel, you do NOT want this one. She's lazy. She's always late. She wears her clothes way too tight. She talks too much. She thinks she knows it all. Trust me. I'm about to fire...'. I interrupted and told her that I didn't appreciate her phone call.

I was clear that I would choose my team, that I didn't need her negative opinions, and that she should have found out why this person seemed to be challenged with prioritizing her time. What if she had offered to have a fun, professional fashion show with her team or taken a few minutes to listen to what she had to say? I abruptly ended the call. Stephanie came in later that day for an interview. I held a group interview. I needed to see what each of their strengths were, how they interacted with each other, who my potential leaders were, who my people-people were, who my numbers-people were, and who my behind-the-scenes people were. I needed to see them as people, not potential candidates.

'Hi. I'm Stephanie and I'm pregnant!' were the very first words out of her mouth. We all erupted in laughter after that first moment of awkward silence. We became a team, a family who spent years in awkwardly hilarious moments!

Stephanie, as every one of my team members did, had unique talents. She was a top-performing sales person out of 11 offices month after month, year after year. Her customers *would drive by four of our other company offices so Stephanie could serve them. They would wait in line for 20 minutes to work with her while there was no line at other stations. How did one manager see so much dirt? She looked for it! During that interview, I asked Stephanie what she loved about her work. She said, 'Talking.' Again, we laughed after the awkward silence.*

Stephanie was a crowd pleaser. She was a problem-solver. She had a natural ability to see a challenge that her customers may have and offer a solution before they even knew there was a potential problem. (The 'she talks too much and thinks she knows it all' dirt.) I asked Stephanie, 'What do you dislike about your job?' I should mention that Stephanie is brutally honest. She said, 'Being at work by 7:30 in the morning. I'm pregnant. I'm tired and I don't sleep well right now. I get my best sleep from 5 to 7:00. It's really hard for me to be at work by 7:30. (Stephanie drove an hour to and from work every day.) I'll just tell you. I'm late a lot. I just can't wake up because I've been up most of the night.' (The 'she's lazy and always late' dirt.) I asked if she would like to work from 9 am until 6 pm. She looked shocked. She sat there, mouth open for at least 30 seconds, and finally said, 'Yes! You would really do that for me?!' Stephanie was never late in her five- year career with me.

Another one of my interview questions was, 'What do you want to do after this?' I always enjoyed the puzzled look on their faces. I explained that I was here to support, motivate, and inspire them to achieve their greatest success, to live their dreams. Stephanie was shocked and said, 'I've never thought about it. No one has ever asked me that question.' Stephanie shared with me that she really needed to buy maternity clothes. Her 'regular' clothes had become too tight. She didn't have the money to purchase new clothes. Especially with a new baby on the way. (The 'she wears her clothes too tight' dirt.) We immediately began working on different ways for Stephanie to access her strengths, increase her skillset, and earn more money. She felt valued. She was motivated. She shined. We found gold. Lots of gold in Stephanie. I looked for the gold, and Stephanie was more valuable than gold will ever be."

-Crystel, VA

Lead me to share my ideas.

Remember, I am your front line, bottom line, and everything in between. I see ways to improve systems, increase profits, gain market share, and retain customers and employees. I have ideas that, if developed, could make you a trend-setter in your industry. Squash my ideas and I will take them elsewhere.

Lead me by serving me.

A leader is a servant of all and above all, not the greatest of all. Ensure that my needs are met. Set clear expectations. Allow me to do what I do best every day. Give me the tools I need to do my job right. Motivate me. Inspire me. Serve me.

If you continuously ask how you can serve me, I will serve your company beyond your expectations.

Lead me by encouraging my work-life integration.

Remember, I cannot balance my work with my life. Allow me to bring my quirks to the office, my unique dance moves, and encourage my personality to shine. Give me the opportunity to connect with my family during working hours. Don't tell me to "check it at the door." I will try to follow this demand, and because it's not possible, I will fail. I am connected and need to know my family is doing well throughout the day. I need the ability to make appointments during work hours for myself and my family. I will not "check it at the door." I will find a way to reach out to my family, to make appointments, and to attend family functions at your cost. I may call in sick. I may have other employees cover for me. I may deliberately do things to get back what I believe is the time you have taken from me and my family.

Allow me to integrate my life into my work and I will flourish with a sense of gratitude to you and your company. My family and I will sing your praises. I will be more productive and give you a greater return on your investment in me.

Lead me with fun!

Work can and should be fun. Zappos™10 has a *culture* of fun. One of their culture points is: "Have fun and create a little weirdness!" Fun is deeply engrained in their culture. We all have fun in separate ways. Ask me how I could bring fun to the workplace. I have great ideas. I may even be willing to create and lead a "fun committee" to ensure that WE have a culture of fun, a place where our employees and customers rave about their fun experiences.

Lead me with empowerment.

You hired me to do a job, to help you achieve your vision. Limit me with policy, procedure, and hierarchy and I will feel my opinions don't matter. I will see that you do not trust my judgment, that you do not trust me. Without trust, I will lose confidence in myself. I will become repeatedly frustrated when I know that I can overcome a challenge on my own, yet constantly need your approval. Encourage me to do my job by using *my* best practices. Encourage me to share with you my ideas that will allow me to do my job even better. Lead me by giving me the opportunity to practice discretion. I know the customers and their needs, and I know your policies and practices. I possess the discretionary savvy needed to combine the two and make decisions that reflect your strong leadership!

Lead me by celebrating me.

I have set milestones that I will achieve in my life. Celebrate my birthdays, my anniversaries, my children's accomplishments, and my contributions to our community. There are multiple facets of my life that require celebration. Celebrate with me and I will create and celebrate your wins with you.

Lead me by learning.

I am ever-evolving and developing as an employee, as should you as a leader. The pianist learns, practices, and hones their skills for an average of 17 and a half years before reaching their greatest potential. At the age of 87, Michelangelo said, "I am still learning.[11]" Continue to learn and practice leadership skills and I will admire you, follow you, and lead by your example. Never stop learning, and you will inspire me to lead even more team members who will follow in my (and your) footsteps.

Lead me with feedback.

Ask me how *you* are doing as a leader. Ask me what you could do to be a better leader. Take my feedback and suggestions to heart. Remember, I want a successful leader to follow. Practice humility and I will share with you what I truly believe will make you a better leader, and me a better employee.

Lead me with responsibility.

Trust me. I know you're not perfect. I don't expect you to be. Be honest and transparent with me about your abilities, strengths, weaknesses, and challenges. Admit to me when you're wrong. Take ownership of your mistakes and I will take ownership of mine. We can work together to learn and grow from our mistakes.

"I was their sales rep and they were making me look bad by not delivering what I was promising. I quit."

-Juliet, MA

Lead me by example.

I need your actions to match your words. It's so simple. Yet, many managers struggle to truly recognize and act on this. If you ask something of me, shouldn't I expect it of you? If you ask me to stay a little late to wrap up a project, wouldn't you offer to stay a little late with me? If you ask me to believe in the core values of your company, wouldn't you show me examples of those core values in your behavior? Ask me to be a team player and I'll expect for you to show up to, and participate in, every practice and game, and celebrate every win as I, your team member would. Please don't ever tell me, "That's not my job as a manager." Remember, *your* job is to lead me.

Leadership is all action. If you see leadership as only a role with authority and operate as THE authority, I will quit. Remember what happens when I quit? I can take your other employees, your customers, and your good-standing online reputation with me.

"As I continued my career in banking, I soon looked for more opportunities within the same career path. I became employed with a large credit union and was flattered by the company and what they had to offer. As time went on, I was able to learn and become very knowledgeable in many areas

of the company only to be led by a leader who was not a leader at all. When I wanted to learn and reach for the stars, there was no support or guidance. How could I succeed if my manager comes to work for a paycheck? How is that fair to me? Because I wanted certain hours, I was stuck with a certain manager who had no interest in his staff moving on to bigger and better opportunities. It wasn't long before I began to feel like a number. I didn't want to go to work, and soon was giving my notice. The company lost a great employee because my leader showed no skills in leadership or motivation. I learned that anytime I interviewed, it was then going to be not only about the company, but the people as well. I can do any job. It's who I am willing to do it for at this point."

-Stephanie, WV

"My manager, Crystel, has always been an excellent leader. A lot of things she shared with me have remained strong and resonated such a deeper meaning. I've been so lucky to have her as a mentor and friend. She inspired by example, not by simply telling. That passion, living by example is what sticks with people. It inspires them to do more. It inspires them to think outside of the box; yes, I could do my basic job description, but what can I do to make a difference too? What can I do that is more, that is within my realm and wheelhouse, and pushes me so that I can grow? What kind of difference can I make for my coworkers, for my customers, and ultimately for myself too? It's all interconnected in deep ways. Crystel told me there was never a task too small, like

filing. We all are in this together. We all have a common goal. I love her!"

-Lisa, VA

I am your employee. Lead me, with fun, motivation, learning, celebrating, serving, responsibility, feedback, empowerment, sharing, and work-life integration! Look for the gold and lead by example! I will do all those contagious things with my coworkers, your customers, and my family too!

Know Me

I want to sincerely thank you for taking the time to uncover my unique abilities, for choosing to develop and challenge me, and for making opportunities to express your appreciation of me. You've done an excellent job fostering my development at work and, for that, I thank you. Now, may I bring one more challenge to you?

I want you to know me, really know me. I don't expect you to be a best friend or a shoulder to cry on. I do need you to understand this truth: My work is a *part* of my life. And because it's a part, and not an equal, I will never be able to "balance" the two. Now, I know what you're thinking. You've read so many articles on work-life balance, it must be possible, right? In fact, your parents probably taught you that work is work and everything outside of work needs to do exactly that, stay outside of work. My parents taught me the same thing! I'm brave enough to challenge them, so I'll challenge you too!

I remember going through a drive-through restaurant with my dad. He's a Baby Boomer by the way (and has quite the traditional separation of work and life philosophy). There was a young employee walking back inside after personally delivering an order to a waiting customer. As she was walking, she was also texting. My dad said, "That's stealing time from your employer!" While I respect and value my dad's remarkable practice of integrity, I offered an alternative perspective. This young woman, a Millennial, lives and breathes thanks to her cell phone! Her way of doing "life" is filled with constant and instant connection. Chatting with her friends, and experiencing an ongoing sense of connection with others, was literally in the palm of her hands. And she's not alone! I love having my phone with me. In fact, I bet you feel like something's missing if you've forgotten yours at home. Technology gives us immediate access to the three things every person needs: belonging, accomplishment, and appreciation. Remember when we talked about that a while back? I need these things at work, for certain, AND I need them from my friends, family, and community who are not at work with me. To keep that need fulfilled in all areas, I am never truly able to "disconnect" from the world outside of work. And you don't want me to. Here's why:

Know my need to stay connected.

If you give me the flexibility to stay connected with my life outside of work, while I'm at work, I will perform for you in ways that will impress! Worrying about something going on with a loved one, for example, will distract me from my work duties. I will never be able to "shut it off" or "check it at the door." Don't ask me to. You've given me crystal clear expectations at work. I am achieving above and beyond those expectations and will continue to do so. Let me check personal emails, or receive personal phone calls. Let me check social media (I might even say a nice word about you!). I need to stay connected to my world. And because my world includes work, you can guarantee that I will stay connected there as well. I asked you to reward me with pay for my performance, not simply for being present. Allow me to incorporate my life into my work while maintaining your expectations of me. I have the power to do both!

"My boss ENCOURAGES us to be on social media while we're at work! I love that I can have my cell phone and chat with my friends and family all day if I want to. It makes me want to post great stuff about my boss and my company, which I do all day too. He only has two rules. Get your job done every day and never put a virtual person before one of your customers. We even take turns watching for customers, so we can put our phones down before they walk in. This is such a fun place to work!"

-Brittany, MD

Know my life.

When you ask me about my life, it makes me want to work harder for you. One reason I will be highly engaged is knowing that my direct supervisor or boss cares about me as a person. We can establish boundaries. I don't need to share all of life's intimacies. I do need you to know about my family, what's going on with them, and need you to ask about them. I need you to know about my life goals and help me be accountable for reaching them. Invest in me on a personal level. Know me. And I'll be your strongest employee.

"There was no personal connection with the company. So, it was just a job and I was just an employee ID number. My boss didn't even know how many kids I have or their names, or even cared. In my five years, he (or his emissaries) never offered to have lunch or an after-work drink with me. I finally quit today."

-Aaron, VA

"The best manager I have ever had also turned out to be the one I, myself, attempt to pattern my behavior as a manager after. In a nutshell, she understood that the person coming to work each day had dreams, goals, feelings and a life outside of the office.

Just before I finished law school, I received a clerkship with three federal judges. I was ecstatic to have gotten the job – and nervous. All three had personalities that were as different as night and day. The work was extremely difficult, but I did well and felt they all trusted my judgement. Over time, most of the work I did was not even checked by them. That made me proud, that made me confident, that reinforced why I had decided on the profession in the first place. But then came the bar exam. In addition to working 50 hours a week, studying for the bar, I had taken on a second law degree program, an, LL.M., masters of law in finance.

In retrospect, it was too much. Anyone and likely everyone could see that, but I was adamant I wanted to get it all over and done with. Nothing and no one could have talked me out of it.

Through the entire process, Judge Terry cheered me on. Every day in chambers she would ask, 'How are you?' – not 'How is the studying coming along,' or, 'How are classes?' She reinforced her focus was me, how I was doing, if I had enough support and rest. This was shocking to me. She was such an accomplished lawyer and judge, the fact she took the time to check on me gave me confidence, shaping how I began to treat and look at my fellow co-workers.

When the time came to take the bar, I missed passing it by 14 points. It was devastating. I didn't want to go to work. Everyone was so excited for me and I knew it would be embarrassing for us all. I was so annoyed and irritated with myself.

I remember walking into court that morning and Judge Terry immediately called a recess and motioned for me to join her in chambers. I told her the results, and after three days of holding back tears, I started sobbing. She sat with me and became the embodiment of a rock in that moment.

'Amy Marie, 60% of the people taking that bar never pass it. You have forgotten all the things those people never even knew in the first place. Fourteen measly points out of 2000? When you take it next time we will celebrate two things: your law license AND your LL.M. - period.'

And I believed her. She was right. I went on to accomplish both. But years later, I often wonder how I did that – it was an insane plan to take it all on. In retrospect, I know beyond a shadow of a doubt it was her faith in me that at some point planted the seed of faith in myself.

When a manager sees not just their worker in the 'now', but rather sees the potential of what they will become, that is what makes an amazing manager – they literally can change the path an employee takes in life.

Ten years and several jobs later, I still talk to Judge Terry on a regular basis. My story is not unique to me – every person that has worked for her has had the same experience. She is a unique person and I am fortunate that my path and career passed her chamber doorstep. To this day, I attempt to emulate her in all I do."

-Amy, NC

"Inflexibility and malicious undertones! My husband and I were both with our company for 7 years. When we had our first child, they refused to work with us. My husband and I were on opposing schedules and right before our son was born, they forced him to resign. We didn't know what we'd do. Once my husband secured a position at another company, I resigned. How can you continue to work for a place like that? It took me about 6 years to realize that I could make a business out of childhood experiences (my parents owned a foodservice and I just started my own!) It's been a better opportunity than I could ever have gotten at that place."

-Wendy, MD

Know my need for open communication.

The more restrictions you place on me, the more likely I am to do what I want to do anyway. I realize this is blunt. I respect you enough to share the truth. As I said earlier, it is impossible to pull "life" out of work. If you implement rules that try to make that possible, I'm going to be irritated and distant, which will manifest in low performance. Also, I'm saving you from unnecessary frustration. Trying to force people to do the impossible will leave you feeling powerless and stressed. Instead, open the lines of communication. Ask about me. Ask about my life. Then, I will be an open book and we will have the most desperately needed element in a workplace: Trust.

"I asked my boss for a day off after working there for about 12 months. I was one of seven people on his team. Any of the other six could have easily covered my day off. He declined my request. I really wanted to go on a field trip with my son. I hadn't been able to be on any of my children's field trips in the year that I had been working there. I didn't think it was too much to ask. Apparently, he did. I couldn't afford to lose my job. I was a single mom of two. So, I decided that I would just call in sick. He couldn't write me up for that. I called in sick every time I wanted to do something fun with my children after that. As a matter-of-fact, I called in any time the weather was nice or I just didn't feel like working. It's sad when I think about it now. I was a great employee. I hadn't missed one day in a year. After that day, I missed a few days per month. Not because I needed to, but because I was angry

that he didn't care about me or my children to give me one day. I finally quit and went to work for their competitor. The first thing I said in my interview was I need to be able to have time with my children throughout the work week. And I do get lots of time with my children. This company is all about family! My children are much older now, but I'll probably retire from this company!"

-Angela, IL

"My employee came to work without panty hose. I was the enforcer of the rules. After all, I was their manager. So, that's what I did. I asked her to come into my office and proceeded to reinforce the dress code policy with her. I thought I did it in a kind way. I asked why she decided to come to work without pantyhose when she clearly knew that it was not in line with our company's dress code policy. She said that she didn't have any. Our office was in a shopping center that contained several retail shops. I told her to clock out and go get a pair of pantyhose. That's exactly what she did. She clocked out and came back two hours later. When I asked where she had been, she said she went to get panty hose. I asked what had taken her two hours? (The shops were in the same parking lot as our office.) She said, 'It takes me an hour to get home and an hour to get back.'

I was in shock. Why would she drive all the way home when she could have walked next door to buy panty hose? She shared with me that she did go next door. The panty hose was $3.00. She did not have $3.00. She went home and borrowed a pair of her mother's panty hose. She changed my *life that day. I apologized, went to the store, and personally bought anything and everything that I thought may interfere with my employees being able to do their job according to the company's dress code. I bought panty hose, scarves, pins, hair brushes, hair spray, soap, you name it. I created a space in our employee break room for them to access any of the items whenever they needed to, without question. I realized that day that panty hose did not make her a better employee. Her heart, talents, and attitude toward our work family made her a phenomenal employee."*

-Crystel, VA

Let me know you.

I want to know about you too. You're not just a boss to me. I choose to work with you because you've dedicated your time to care about me at work. The more I know about you, the more I can like you, trust you, and respect you. You don't have to take me up on this. Just know that I believe the success of any business is founded in relationships. That includes ours. So, help me become your number one ambassador!

"I remember the first time I saw my boss cry. I couldn't believe it! She was human! I don't know why but I walked in her office, sat in the chair facing her desk, and just stared at her with compassion. To my surprise she shared her life with me that day. She was crying because she had just found out that her daughter was going to study abroad, and she was concerned for her safety. She was her only child after three miscarriages, and she was a single mother. Just seeing her in

such a vulnerable state made her human. It made her like my mom. We talked for about half an hour that day. It forever changed our relationship and quite honestly my loyalty to her and our company."

-Jessica, MA

Now, back to the young server at the restaurant. My guess is that her employer understands her audience (her employees). She understands the importance of caring about her team. She gets that life doesn't stop when you clock in. She knows that her team will serve her well, because she is looking out for them. It really is that simple. Know your team. Know me. Know that we will pull out all the stops for you when you do the same for us.

The Numbers

If after reading this book, you still don't believe that it's all about **me**, let me give you a few statistics based on over 25 years of research with millions of employees, that may finally convince you.

According to Gallup's® latest State of the American Workplace report, 51% of the American workforce is actively looking for a new job. Let that sink in for a moment. That means that potentially over half of *your* employees are looking for a new job as we speak. I'm sure you're thinking, "They just want more money." That couldn't be further from the truth. The number one reason over half of all working Americans are looking for a new job is, and I quote, "to have the opportunity to do what they do best every day." As a matter of fact, it out ranked pay by four times! Convinced yet?

Numbers matter to you, I know. How about a few more? Gallup's® research also proved that my engagement in your organization directly affects your four key business outcomes. I, your employee, if fully engaged, can increase your profits by as much as 21%. I'll give you a moment to do that math. I can also increase productivity by 20%. What are the possibilities for your company if I were 20% more productive every day? What if I told you that I, your employee, also have the power to increase your customer loyalty by 10%? Imagine if you retained 10% more customers year after year! That's a compound effect that provides a massive return on your investment.

As for that 51% of people looking for a new job, I can make a difference. I can decrease your turnover by 24-49%! What does it cost you to attract, hire, train, and ultimately lose one employee? Take a moment to calculate what a 24-49% reduction in turnover would mean to your bottom line. Not to mention the overall morale of your company.

Remember when I told you that I would find other ways to integrate my life into my work with things like calling in sick? According to Gallup®, I can also reduce absenteeism by as much as 49%! What if I, your employee, took half of the number of days off that I do now? Talk about an impact on profitability, productivity, and customer loyalty!

The Commitment

Now, I hope that you see it *is* all about me, your employee. You must take the time to teach me, and teach me again. Show me that you appreciate me. Value me as the asset I am. Include me in your vision. Discover and develop me personally and professionally. Tailor my role to my strengths. Equip me with the tools I need. Measure my success. Reward me for my contributions. Lead me to success. Finally, know me as a person who has a life, of which work is merely a part and in turn I will make it all about *you*!

I'm committed to you. Will you commit to me?

Here's your opportunity:

I, _____, commit to teaching, appreciating, valuing, discovering, developing, tailoring, equipping, measuring, rewarding, and knowing you!

Signature: _____

Date: _____

Source Notes

1. Chapman, G. (2004). *The Five Love Languages: How to Express Heartfelt Commitment to Your Mate.* Chicago, IL: Northfield Publishing.

2. Chapman, G. & White, P. (2012). *The 5 Languages of Appreciation in the Workplace: Empowering Organizations by Encouraging People.* Chicago, IL: Northfield Publishing.

3. Buckingham, M. & Clifton, D.O. (2001). Now Discover Your Strengths. New York, NY: The Free Press.

4. Gallup®. www.gallup.com

5. Rath, T. (2007). *Strengths Finder 2.0.* New York, NY: Gallup Press

6. Chapman, G. & White, P. (2012). *Motivating by Appreciation (MBA) Inventory.*

7. DISC® Classic 2.0 (2003). Inscape Publishing.

8. (2017). Gallup®. www.gallup.com

9. Heasley, K. (April 10, 2015). *Heasley & Partners, Inc., Facebook status update.* https://www.facebook.com/heasleyandpartners/posts/10152939248732655

10. (2017). Zappos®. www.zappos.com

11. (2017). www.brainyquote.com

12. (2016). State of the American Workplace. www.gallup.com